# Contents

# Japanese Costume and Textile Arts

# Japanese Costume and Textile Arts

*by* SEIROKU NOMA

translated by Armins Nikovskis

New York · WEATHERHILL / HEIBONSHA · Tokyo

This book was originally published in Japanese by Heibonsha under the title *Kosode to No-isho* in the Nihon no Bijutsu series.

A full glossary-index covering the entire series will be published when the series is complete.

*First English Edition, 1974*

*Jointly published by John Weatherhill, Inc., 149 Madison Avenue, New York, New York 10016, with editorial offices at 7-6-13 Roppongi, Minato-ku, Tokyo 106, and Heibonsha, Tokyo.*  *Printed in Japan.*

LCC Card No. 74–76781

ISBN 0-8348-1026-3

# Japanese Costume and Textile Arts

# Volume 16

## THE HEIBONSHA SURVEY OF JAPANESE ART

*For a list of the entire series see end of book*

### CONSULTING EDITORS

CHAPTER ONE

# The Kimono and Its Setting

THE EVOLUTION OF a distinctive national mode of dress is a long, cumulative process, all the more so in the case of a national costume that is artistically outstanding. Japan, of course, has been culturally influenced by both the East and the West. Yet its national costume, the kimono, is quite different from those of the West, and indeed is a unique form of dress even in the East. Why is it, then, that Japan has developed such a distinctive garment? To answer this question we will have to look at the course of formation of Japanese culture itself.

LAND AND CLIMATE Dress is greatly influenced by everyday life. However beautiful it may be, if it is inconvenient for daily life, it will not be put to practical use. And daily life in Japan is closely related to the country's climatic and geographical features. In the first place, it is conditioned by the warm, humid climate. The dress form that evolved in Japan is neither the enclosed type common to cold regions nor the open type of hot regions, but an intermediate type. The reason for this is the requirement of airiness in order to counter humidity. Wide sleeves and wraparound skirts were therefore desirable. The art of constructing wooden-framed buildings also developed because of climatic considerations, and the Japanese came to feel a sense of well-being in sitting on the floor. When working, the Japanese assume whatever attitude is suitable for the activity in hand, like everybody else, but when relaxing they like to sit or kneel on the floor. This preference is not at all peculiar to the Japanese, but in the case of stone or brick buildings, the fact that the materials are hard and cold to the touch rules out sitting on the floor itself. However, the people of some nations are still able to do this by putting some kind of carpet or matting on the floor.

A loose, comfortable style of dress like the kimono is essential for freedom of movement in this mode of life, and the kimono is thus the result of a long accumulation of experience. In early times Japan also had a period when dress of the Western pattern, consisting of separate upper and lower garments, was worn, but this was probably developed under the influence of dress styles on the Asian continent (Figs. 1, 2, 3, 4). In the Nara period (646–794), the influence received from Chinese culture of the T'ang dynasty (618–907) was particularly strong, and the Japanese must have imitated China's advanced mode of dress. But their climate and way of life would not allow the Japanese to follow continental styles indefinitely, and so they sought a form of clothing more suited to their circumstances.

JAPANESE-STYLE DRESS The uniqueness of the kimono is not due to Japan's isolation from other civilizations. It is the result of working out what is appropriate to the climate and life of the Japanese while fully aware

1. Lady Under a Tree. *Detail from a screen painting. Eighth century. Shoso-in, Nara.*

*2 (opposite page, left). Lady under a tree. Detail of T'ang painting excavated at Astana. Eighth century. Atami Art Museum, Shizuoka Prefecture.* ▷

*3 (opposite page, right). Figurine of lady. T'ang three-color ware. Eighth century.* ▷

of other forms of dress and so has a positive cultural value. Again, however unique it may be, unless it is also aesthetically pleasing, it is not worthy of a nation's pride. The kimono's ability to stand up to this kind of appraisal is due to the fact that while adopting many elements from outside, the Japanese were not overwhelmed by these but developed a form of dress to suit their own environment.

A typically Japanese dress style was more or less formed by the tenth century. However, it had not been able to free itself completely from T'ang influence and in any case was restricted to the nobility. It was not until about the thirteenth century that what we now think of as characteristically Japanese clothes spread to the general populace, and it was then that the two forms of clothing that can be said to have given birth to the kimono flourished. These are the type of garment known as the *kosode* (literally, "small sleeves") and the costumes of the Noh theater.

In fact not only did these two forms give birth to the kimono, but they themselves exhibit the full beauty of the kimono. The most important reason for this is that Noh costume was nurtured under the patronage of the aristocracy and as part of a stage art of refined sensibility. It matured in fortunate surroundings, and the appearance of costumes outstanding both functionally and artistically was due to the existence of this environment. The kosode represents a popularization of Noh costume and is its worthy heir.

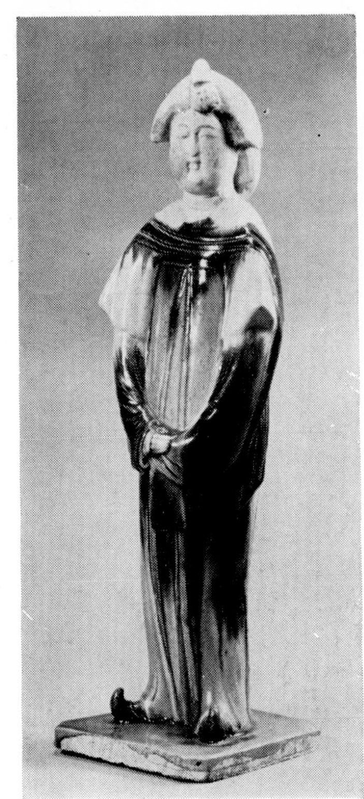

## THE BEAUTY OF THE KIMONO

However intensely the Japanese may have felt a need for a truly Japanese style of clothing, if there had been no moving force to energize this desire, it could not have been realized. Such a moving force is even more important when it comes to evolving something of artistic value—here enlightened patronage is required. Noh costume and the kosode had the backing of wealthy daimyo and merchants, and the perfected beauty of the garments gave pleasure to their patrons. The tradition of patronage remains today of course, but dress cannot find the kind of financial support enjoyed in the Edo period (1603–1868; also known as the Tokugawa period). Noh costume and kosode developed in the right age and the right environment. And the modern kimono is the flower that has blossomed from these roots. It is surely proper that people see in the kimono a beauty of great artistic value. There is good reason for the admiration the kimono enjoys abroad nowadays.

Although most national costumes resemble each other to some degree, they are worn with pride on festive occasions. The Japanese, however, are not proud of their kimono. Instead they regard it as a burden left over from the old Japan. The kimono is said to be unsuited to an active life and to hide the beauty of the human body. But clothing is not worn for utility alone. Comfortable clothing for relaxation is also necessary. So is clothing for special occasions, and the people of many nations are proud to wear festive dress that is inconvenient for

*4. Portrait of Crown Prince Shotoku with two young princes. Late seventh or early eight century. Imperial Household Collection.*

most forms of activity. To think of clothes only in terms of efficiency is to disregard the human element. If people have to work, they also have to play.

The complaint is often heard that the kimono hides the beauty of the body. It is undeniable that the kimono covers the body, and its simplified shape does blur the body's subtle undulations. But this criticism is based on the premise that the nude is the acme of human beauty. If we take this point of view, where does the relatively form-fitting Western type of dress stand? Is it not true that it seeks to achieve the beauty of the naked form, paradoxically enough, by enclosing the body to an even greater extent than does the kimono? Neither overexposing nor unduly covering the body, the kimono allows one to appreciate the body's beauty allusively. While it may be that this glorification of the kimono stands in opposition to the adoration of the nude, there are people who admire the kimono-clad body. Since the kosode and Noh costume are the sources from which the kimono's beauty springs, I want now to consider them here in some detail.

CHAPTER TWO

# Rise of the Kosode

Kosode is an old name for the form of dress that is now usually simply called kimono. The name is said to have come into use in the Kamakura period (1185–1336), when the robe that had been worn by nobles of the Heian period (794–1185) as an underkimono began to be worn as an outer garment because it permitted greater freedom of movement. Kosode literally means "small sleeves" and is used in contrast with the terms *hirosode* and *osode* (literally, "wide sleeves" and "large sleeves," respectively). It would perhaps be advisable to define the terms "length" and "width" as used in connection with kimono sleeves, as they may otherwise be the cause of some confusion to the Western reader. If we imagine the arm stretched out horizontally, the dimension from the shoulder to the outer end of the sleeve we shall call the length, while the dimension from the top to the bottom of the sleeve we shall call the width, although this dimension is often larger than the length. In the case of garments of the *hirosode* type, the sleeve end is left entirely open (Fig. 67), whereas in the kosode, the lower part of the end is sewn up, leaving only a relatively narrow opening. (In Figure 41 the red lining of the kosode can be seen at the upper part of the sleeve, where it is open.) In fact, garments of the kosode type usually have sleeves that are both narrower and shorter than the sleeves of *hirosode* garments, but the real criterion is the extent of the opening. This is apparent when we consider the type of garment known as *furisode* (literally, "swinging sleeves"; Fig. 6). According to the definition of width given above, this garment has extremely wide sleeves (although we would normally think of them as long), and it might at first sight seem appropriate to classify it as a *hirosode* or *osode* garment. But a closer look (Fig. 112) discloses that only about a quarter of the sleeve width is open, the rest having been sewn up, and the *furisode* is in fact technically regarded as a special type of kosode.

Wide sleeves of the *hirosode* type held a great attraction for the Heian-period nobleman. Although they required a great deal of material, their form was beautiful and elegant, and they were considered ideal for the aristocracy. In harmony with the wide sleeves, the skirts of garments were long. This must have been inconvenient for working, but this was the dress of wealthy people in a wealthy age, people for whom work was not a necessity. Not unnaturally, their style was imitated by the common people. Records of the period show that edicts limiting the width of sleeves were issued a number of times, indicating not only how popular wide sleeves were but also that the edicts were quickly ignored.

Even in this age of glorification of the wide sleeve, the poor had to be satisfied with narrow sleeves. On a late-Heian "fan sutra" (Fig. 16) showing scenes of the everyday life of the period, girl street vendors and shopgirls are shown wearing clothes with narrow sleeves. Thus when the term "kosode" began to be used for the underrobes worn

5. *Detail of kosode (Korin Kosode). Design of autumn plants on white ground, hand-painted by Ogata Korin. About 1700 (mid-Edo period). Tokyo National Museum.*

6. Furisode. *Figured satin;* yuzen *dyed design of stylized bundle of* noshi *(dried strips of abalone, considered auspicious) on red ground. Seventeenth or eighteenth century (mid-Edo period). Yuzen History Society, Kyoto.* ▷

by the nobility, narrow sleeves still had associations of low social status, and it was only later, when the kosode had developed into formal, festive wear, that the word took on the connotation of something charming or pretty.

## THE KOSODE REVOLUTION

How this revolutionary change in the status of the kosode came about is a fascinating story. Women's attachment to their clothes is deep-rooted in any age or culture, and it is impossible to bring about any radical change in clothing styles unless there is considerable motivation. In the Heian period the so-called *juni-hitoe* (literally, "twelve unlined robes") fashion was developed to replace the Chinese style of women's dress. This was a revolutionary development, and the reasons for it are to be seen in the great change represented by the transfer of the capital from Nara to Kyoto, and the refinement of courtly life centered on the ruling Fujiwara clan.

Let us now consider the reasons for the kosode's rise to popularity. Probable contributing factors that immediately come to mind are the final defeat of the powerful Taira family by the Minamoto clan in 1185, marking the beginning of the Kamakura period and the transfer of political power from the nobility to the military samurai class and, accompanying this, the eclipse of the "Kyoto style" of the capital by the "Eastern style" of the new seat of actual power in the east, Kamakura. And although the government in later times issued numerous sumptuary edicts concerning dress, it seems unlikely that the Kamakura government would have issued one especially to institute a new form of attire for women. The popularity of the kosode was more probably due to spontaneous imitation of the fashions of the governing class.

*7. Detail from* Shigi-san Engi Emaki *(Legends of Shigi-san Temple Picture Scroll). Second half of twelfth century. Chogosonshi-ji, Nara.*

Essentially, the creed of the samurai, the new ruling class, urged a life of simplicity and frugality. The gorgeous attire of court ladies, unsuited to an active life, was impractical, and was indeed considered improper for women of samurai families. The house of Taira ignored the warrior's creed and as a result weakened, eventually meeting with disaster. The new rulers, the Minamoto clan, took care not to repeat this mistake. In fact the reason they governed the country from the Kanto area in the east of Japan was that they feared they might otherwise be corrupted by the *Kyo-fu,* or "Kyoto style." Although we have no surviving example to tell us what kind of clothes the ladies of the Kanto samurai families wore, depictions in picture scrolls do tell us a little.

The dress of samurai women was in principle simple, although it seems unlikely that it could have been all that simple once the samurai class had obtained a certain amount of power at the end of the Heian period. The wide-sleeved robe worn by a female retainer of the "rich man of Yamazaki" in the *Legends of Shigi-san Temple* picture scroll (Fig. 7), for example, is not merely an undergarment. And in the Muromachi period (1336–1568), when Japan was also under the rule of the warrior class, the *Legends of Seiko-ji* picture scroll shows rather elaborate clothes. So although members of the samurai class led simple lives, the kosode was gradually gaining the colorful characteristics beloved of women. We can surmise this from Noh costumes for female roles, as these are believed to represent the dress of samurai women of the period.

The samurai, in their new status as rulers, were

8. *Kimono and* hakama *on a stand; detail from a* tagasode byobu *(garment screen). Seventeenth century (early Edo period).*

9. *Kosode.* Dan-gawari *allover design of embroidered bamboo grass and paulownia, cherry, and wisteria blossoms and leaves. Second half of sixteenth century (Momoyama period).*

*10. Kosode. Glossed silk; design of flowers and grasses in gold leaf and embroidery. Second half of sixteenth century (Momoyama period).*

◁ *11. Kosode. White figured satin; design of irises by a stream. Seventeenth or eighteenth century (mid-Edo period). Nagao Art Museum, Tokyo.*

*12. Kosode. White figured satin; design of wisterias, floral medallions, and rocks in* kanoko *tie-dyed spots and embroidery. Seventeenth century (mid-Edo period). Ohiko Textile Art Research Institute, Tokyo.*

13. *Noh costume* (atsuita). Dan-gawari *design of checks and* karakusa *scrolls. Seventeenth or eighteenth century (mid-Edo period). Noda Shrine, Yamaguchi Prefecture.*

14. *Noh costume* (karaori). *Design of "flaming drum" medallions and peonies. Seventeenth or eighteenth century (mid-Edo period). Nagao Art Museum, Tokyo.*

15. *Noh costume* (nuihaku). *Design of silver-leaf stripes and embroidered bush clover on a white ground. Seventeenth or eighteenth century (mid-Edo period). Okura Cultural Foundation, Tokyo.*

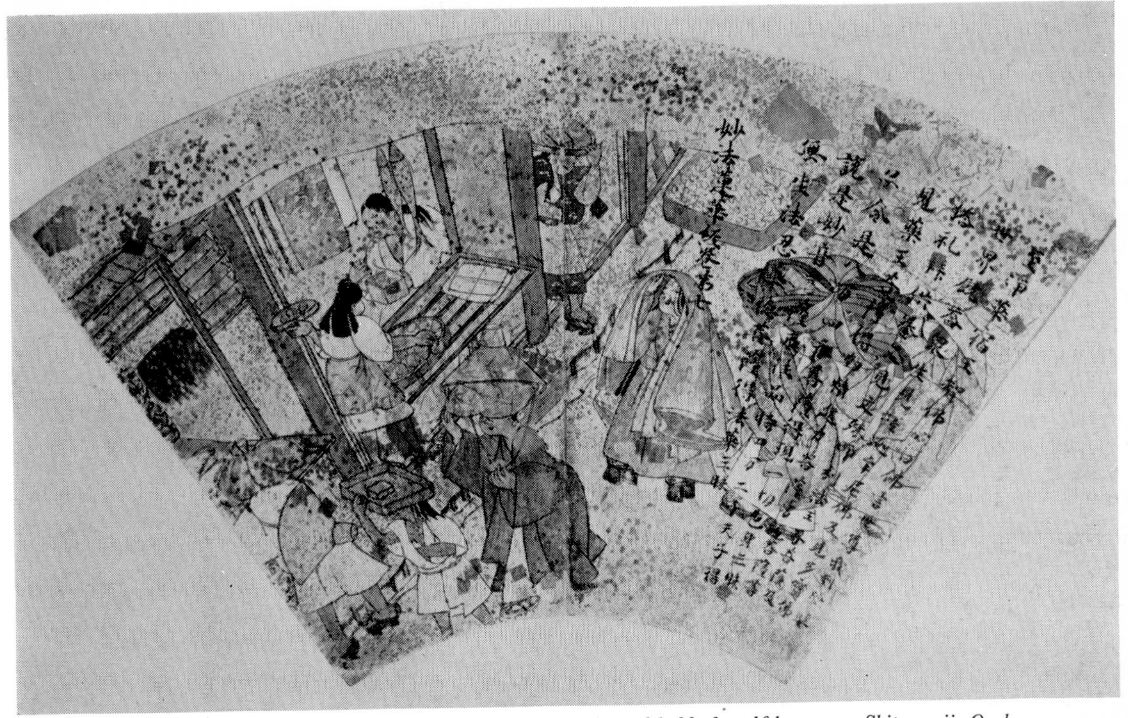

*16. Sutra fan with underpainting showing street scene. Second half of twelfth century. Shitenno-ji, Osaka.*

aware that culturally they were the inferiors of the court nobles, and it is reasonable that they should have wanted to develop their own culture. Since they were not yet in a position to do this alone, they had to imitate the courtiers in some respects. However, with regard to men's dress, the adoption by the samurai of the *eboshi* and *ori-eboshi* caps instead of the courtiers' *kammuri,* and their use of the *suo* robe in place of the courtiers' *ho* were attempts to express their independence. Similarly, we may imagine that samurai women's dress expressed the difference between samurai women and those of the court.

To speak of the beauty of the kosode is to speak of the beauty of the kimono. The kosode style is called *hitoe-gi* (literally, "single-layer wear"), in contrast with the courtly *kasane-gi,* or multilayer style, which it superseded. The court lady's *juni-hitoe* consisted of twelve unlined robes worn one over the other. Each one was simple in color and design, but the aim was a complex beauty at the collar and sleeve openings, where the colors of all twelve robes were visible. These color schemes were termed *kasane no irome* (meaning "color combinations of layered robes"), and great importance was attached to their appropriateness to the season and occasion. In later ages considerable ingenuity was expended on the coloring and design of the underrobes worn with the kosode, but originally beauty was sought by concentrating technique and creativity on the single layer of the outer garment. Thus the simple and relatively unvaried shape of the kosode was complemented by the elaborateness of its surface.

It may seem strange that the early kosode were worn with quite simple obi, or sashes, but it was

commonly thought that an elaborately beautiful obi would in fact detract from the beauty of the kosode. This tradition continued for a surprisingly long time, and until the Edo period the obi was considered relatively unimportant. We can see from this how all attention was concentrated on the kosode itself. The relationship between kosode and obi is seen in a new light when we consider that from the end of the Edo period to the present, more and more interest has been focused on the obi, since the development of the kosode—in form, designs, and techniques—came to a dead end, and designers looked to the obi for new opportunities.

From the beginning to nearly the end of the Edo period the basic form of the kosode remained virtually unchanged, with only slight variations in design. However, complexity and variety were gained by the use of obi in a variety of widths and by varying the position of the knot of the obi—in front, in back, at one side, and so on. One major development was the liberal use of heavy weaves for the obi. Such cloths as tapestry weave and *kinran* and *ginran* (types of gold and silver brocade, respectively) were too stiff and heavy to be used for the kosode but were suitable for the obi. This opened up a vast new world for the development of the kimono in general, but as far as the kosode itself was concerned, its place was being usurped.

Nowadays the obi attracts more attention than the kosode itself. The obi has become so sumptuous that it has become necessary to relate the kosode to it in such a way that the kosode is not overwhelmed by the obi. However, to try to do this by making the kosode vie with the obi in sumptu-

◁ *17. Detail from* Women's Entertainments. *Pair of sixfold screens. About 1630. Yamato Bunkakan, Nara.*

*18. Dyer's shop. Detail from one of a set of paintings of artisans and tradesmen by Kano Yoshinobu, mounted on a pair of sixfold screens. First half of seventeenth century (early Edo period). Kita-in, Saitama Prefecture.*

ousness would result in vulgarity. The kosode design must be restrained so as to balance harmoniously with the extravagant obi. The age when the quest for beauty could be concentrated on the kosode alone is past, although of course many beautiful garments remain as relics of the kosode's age of freedom.

## KOSODE AND FEMININE BEAUTY

The second important point to be considered in connection with the beauty of the kosode is that its development made the most of the physical beauty of Japanese women. In the age when the court had power, when ladies wore *kasane-gi* (layered robes) with long trains, the body was concealed in the inner recesses of the robes and it was no exaggeration to say that beauty of dress constituted female beauty. The *yamato-e* style of painting of the Heian period had an extremely simple formula for representing faces, called *hikime-kagihana* (roughly, "lines for eyes and hooks for noses"). Although there were other reasons for the simplicity of this technique, it does show us how little importance was attached to physical beauty at that time. In contrast with the elaborate *kasane-gi,* the thin kosode showed the soft lines of the body and directed attention to a woman's physical beauty.

If we examine early genre paintings and ukiyo-e prints, we will immediately notice just how painstakingly the artists endeavored to depict the beauty of the female body by means of clothing. Admittedly, the representation is not direct, as in the case of the Western nude, and the draftsmanship is at

*19. Detail from* Yuna *(Bathhouse Girls). Hanging scroll; 1620–30. Atami Art Museum, Shizuoka Prefecture.*

times naive, but the efforts made to indicate physical beauty were extraordinary. In this period, the depiction of the beauty of the female form attained a popularity that has never been equaled. The beginnings of this tendency may perhaps be seen in *Maple Viewing at Mount Takao* (Fig. 25). *Bathhouse Girls* (Fig. 19) is another good example. This development culminated in the work of ukiyo-e artists like Miyagawa Choshun* (1683–1753; Fig. 20) and Kitagawa Utamaro (1753–1806). Of course, all these works principally show the beauty of the kosode, but at the same time they exhibit a deep interest in women's physical beauty. The indirect expression of physical beauty through the medium of clothes suggests excellently the allusive beauty of the Japanese woman.

The coming of the Edo period can be said to have opened the eyes of the Japanese to the beauty of the female body, but another relevant fact that must not be overlooked is that the kosode became the principal item of women's attire. Did this new interest in physical beauty bring on the age of the kosode? Or did the kosode create the interest in women's physical beauty? Either interpretation is possible. The fact is that with the advent of the kosode the Japanese became intoxicated with the mysterious beauty of the female body.

At present, however, when the obi has become such an important part of women's clothing, very little suggestion of a woman's physical beauty re-

* The names of all premodern Japanese in this book are given, as in this case, in Japanese style (surname first); those of all modern (post-1868) Japanese are given in Western style (surname last).

*20.* Courtesan, *by Miyagawa Choshun. Eighteenth century (Edo period). Freer Gallery of Art, Washington.*

21. *Noh costume* (nuihaku). *Design of cherry blossoms on brown ground. Second half of sixteenth century (Momoyama period). Okayama Art Museum, Okayama Prefecture.*

*22 (opposite page, left). Page from kimono design book* (Shinsen On-hiinagata). *1666.* ▷

*23 (opposite page, right). Dancing woman. First half of seventeenth century (early Edo period). Suntory Art Museum, Tokyo.* ▷

mains. People often remark that the young apprentice geisha of Kyoto have a doll-like, inhuman beauty, and indeed the kosode has deteriorated to a very similar state.

## OVERTHROW OF TRADITION

In fifteenth- and sixteenth-century Japan there were many independent lords in various parts of the country who owed their positions to their military prowess. The turnover of rulers was so rapid that no one knew when the so-called age of turbulence would come to an end. In the sixteenth century, however, the generals Oda Nobunaga (1534–82) and Toyotomi Hideyoshi (1536–98) between them unified the country, putting a stop to the long period of civil wars and ushering in an age of peace. With peace and national unity, an age of hedonism ensued. The Momoyama period (1568–1603) was short, but its influence changed the face of Japanese culture. It was this period, because it boldly smashed tradition and allowed free creativity, that made it possible for the unique beauty of the kosode to be realized.

Many of the fetters that had bound the common people fell away with surprising ease in this period. The arrogance of the men who rose to power around the last Ashikaga shoguns at the end of the Muromachi period was one factor tending to destroy the authority of tradition, but the deciding factor was Nobunaga's oppression of Buddhism. Sheltered by special privileges, the Buddhist estab-

lishment had for a long time wielded considerable de facto power, to such a degree that its authority remained unquestioned even by reckless warriors. Nobunaga called the bluff of the Buddhist clergy and dealt it a crushing blow, considering it a hindrance to the unification of the nation. His policy of burning famous temples throughout the country, including that ancient center of pilgrimage, the Enryaku-ji near Kyoto, and slaughtering thousands of priests was the result of his desire to make a clean sweep of those who lived by clinging to the mere forms of tradition.

In the more liberal age following the wars, there was a desire for personal freedom. The newly risen classes were consciously hostile to the old order, and to hide their ignorance of traditional culture, they boldly sought the new and novel. The Momoyama art left today consists mainly of free creations outside the old traditions. For the same reasons, the kosode also developed by leaps and bounds. An age had arrived when those who had succeeded in life, whatever their backgrounds, could freely wear kosode in the city streets. The wives of generals who had become daimyo on the strength of their military abilities started wearing colorful kosode as an expression of the joy of those who had achieved success. In the same manner the women of the wealthy merchant class of Sakai (near modern Osaka) and Hakata (in northern Kyushu), which had amassed vast profits from overseas trade, donned this symbolic garment as an expression of the joy of the wealthy.

*24. Detail of Nembutsu dance from painting of Okuni Kabuki. Seventeenth century (Edo period).*

Widespread acceptance of the kosode was accelerated by entertainers and courtesans. It is the way of the world that such people play a central part in earthly pleasures, and the Japan of the Momoyama period was no exception. About the beginning of the seventeenth century a shrine dancer from Izumo (in the northern part of modern Shimane Prefecture) called Okuni went to Kyoto, and her *kabuki-odori* dances (Fig. 24) overwhelmed the capital. Their bold, innovative movements must have been one reason for this, while the daringly colorful costumes were surely another reason why audiences were captivated. Although the Noh of this period had also become a gorgeous spectacle, it was too sophisticated for the general populace. They liked their entertainments to have a touch of vulgarity, like Okuni's performances.

Prostitution was a way of keeping alive for women who found themselves in reduced circumstances as a result of the wars. The so-called *yuna* (literally, "bathhouse girls") and other kinds of courtesans began to appear in large numbers around this time. The advent of these courtesans was also a natural consequence of the sexual emancipation of the period. In order to attract clients, the women wore kosode of striking design. Most of the kosode of that period left today are garments once worn by members of wealthy families; no example of kosode used by courtesans is extant. Perhaps such garments were used until they were completely worn out. Nevertheless, we can gain some idea of the appearance of courtesans' kosode from contemporary genre paintings. Of course the paintings do not reveal what materials were

25. *Detail from* Maple Viewing at Mount Takao. *Folding screen by Kano Hideyori. Second half of sixteenth century. Tokyo National Museum. (See also Figure 29.)*

26. Dofuku *used by Toyotomi Hideyoshi.* Tsujigahana *dyed design of paulownia leaves and arrows. Late sixteenth century (Momoyama period).*

*27. Detail from folding screen showing the Shijo Riverbed entertainment district in Kyoto. About 1620. Seikado Library, Tokyo.*

used, but they show clearly that the designs were novel and bold. There was nothing to restrict the taste of these free women, as there had been in the case of samurai women of an earlier age.

The daimyo, the rich merchants, and the courtesans of the Momoyama period, representing the three classes of samurai, *chonin* (townspeople, or merchants and artisans), and entertainers, developed their own ideas of the beauty of the kosode, and these ideas influenced one other, resulting in an even greater variety. If we look at depictions of the amusement quarters of the time, such as the *Rakuchu Rakugai Zu* (Scenes In and Around Kyoto) and *Shijogawara Zu* (The Riverbed at Shijo; Fig. 27) folding screens, we can see that the streets are overflowing with people in gorgeous clothing. In all of Japan's long history there is no other period when the streets were so full of color. This was an age when the beauty of the kosode lent a bright accent even to the everyday lives of the common people.

The pleasures of freedom of dress were available not only to women but also to men. Several robes of a type called *dofuku* once worn by such historical figures as Uesugi Kenshin (1530–78), Toyotomi Hideyoshi, and Tokugawa Ieyasu (1542–1616; founder of the Tokugawa shogunate) are extant (Figs. 26, 36). On them the designers have let their fancy run free, producing such colorful designs that one would hardly believe that these garments belonged to famous military leaders. Ieyasu's kosode (Fig. 33), with a tie-dyed indigo pattern of maple leaves, could easily be mistaken for a woman's garment. These are everyday clothes, but the *jim-*

*28. Detail from* Merrymaking Under the Cherry Blossoms. *Pair of folding screens by Kano Naganobu. About 1610. Formerly in Hara Collection, Tokyo. Lost in fire.*

*baori* vests worn on campaign (Fig. 77) are equally extravagant. One wonders what had happened to the traditional temperament of the samurai, who was supposed to prize inner values rather than externals. But there was no reason why the samurai should have been bound by a temperament or disposition traditionally attributed to them. They wanted to experience for themselves the joys that other people savored. They considered that the joy of wearing beautiful clothes should not be restricted to women but should be allowed to men also. In that emancipated age, there were restrictions neither of class nor of sex in regard to clothing. Nor were there distinctions of age—everyone was intoxicated by color.

The kosode is often thought of as a woman's garment, but the term refers to men's garments as well, and both men and women played a part in its development. This is clear from early genre painting. On the screen *Maple Viewing at Mount Takao* (Fig. 29), the men's dress is not especially colorful, but the young man shown in *Merrymaking Under the Cherry Blossoms* (Fig. 28), thought to be Toyotomi Hideyori, Hideyoshi's son, and his attendants are wearing colorful clothes. Genre paintings often show a man surrounded by courtesans, and unless one is careful one is liable not to notice that the figure in the middle is a man, so sumptuous is his costume.

This freedom in the field of dress, however,

*29. Detail from* Maple Viewing at Mount Takao. *Folding screen by Kano Hideyori. Second half of sixteenth century. Tokyo National Museum. (See also Figure 25.)*

lasted only for the duration of the Momoyama period, when tradition had lost its authority and there was neither moral nor social pressure to hold back the free development of costume. Liberty has automatic limits. Pursuit of the same kind of extravagant display by both men and women leads to confusion. And lack of distinction between young and old leads to disrespect. The time had come, early in the seventeenth century, for a conservative reaction.

To stabilize the nation whose reins of power they now held, the leaders of the Tokugawa shogunate in Edo (modern Tokyo) made every effort to stratify society and to perfect the feudal system as quickly as possible. The shogunate emphasized the necessity for people to behave in accordance with their class, the principal distinctions being between the four classes of samurai, farmer, artisan, and merchant. The wearing of dress unsuited to one's station was punished as "behavior lacking in discretion," and society as a whole gradually came to regard such behavior with disapproval. One is struck by the great contrast between this age and the Momoyama period, with its almost unlimited freedom. The prohibitions issued during the Edo period illustrate clearly the process whereby personal freedom was gradually reduced. But even in this repressive age there were some contexts in which a limited freedom remained. These were the licensed quarters and the theater.

30. *Detail from the Hikone Screen. About 1630.*

31. Windblown Beauty, *ukiyo-e painting by Kaigetsudo Ando. Early eighteenth century.*

*32. Kosode. White figured satin; design of scattered fishing nets. Eighteenth century (mid-Edo period). Tokyo National Museum.*

If prostitutes pursued their calling unrestricted, they would inevitably influence their surroundings. Their complete suppression, however, would show a lack of understanding of human nature. The solution of the Edo authorities was to collect the prostitutes into one district and so contain their influence. In this way the licensed pleasure quarters came into being. Although there were other reasons why the quarters flourished during the two hundred and sixty years or so of the Edo period, one is that they provided the only places within a strict feudal society where some freedom was permitted. The fact that the licensed quarters acted as a hothouse for the development of the impractical hair styles of the time, with their ornamental combs and hairpins, is an indication of how eagerly personal adornment was pursued in this island of freedom. The beautiful kosode found there a world in which it could not only survive but also develop in the direction of an increasingly fanciful beauty. The pictures of beauties by artists like the ukiyo-e painter Kaigetsudo Ando (traditionally 1671–1743; Fig. 31) or Miyagawa Choshun (Fig. 20) have caught the charm of the beautiful kosode worn by the courtesans. One is attracted by the brilliant clothes and at the same time made aware of the physical beauty of the women. And this combination is precisely what captured the hearts of those who visited the enticing world of the pleasure quarters.

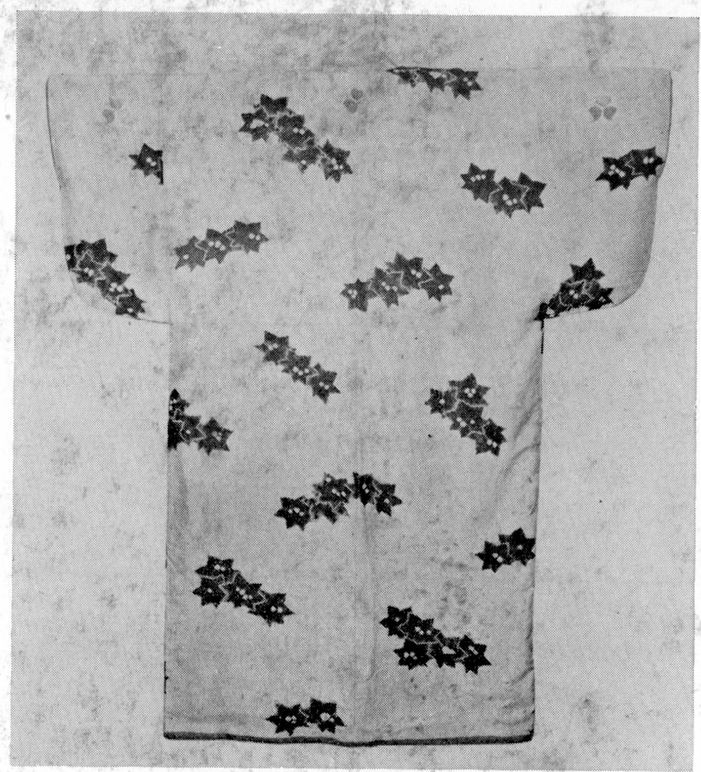

*33. Quilted kosode used by Tokugawa Ieyasu.* Tsujigahana *dyed design of maple leaves. Late sixteenth century (Momoyama period). Tokugawa Art Museum, Nagoya.*

Another area of freedom was the world of theater and dance. People enjoyed seeing on the stage beautiful clothes that could not be worn in the outside world, and producers responded to the public's demand by showing luxurious costumes not permitted in everyday life. Although these costumes helped keep the kosode alive, the pursuit of dramatic effects also led to its becoming an unrealistic "theatrical" dress, with the result that the inherent beauty of the kosode was lost. This corresponds to what happened in the pleasure quarters, where the kosode developed into a special form of dress peculiar to that milieu. However, these two environments were the centers of fashion, and ordinary women secretly copied the designs that originated there. Good examples are the cases of the actor Mizuki Tatsunosuke, who started the fashion for *dandara-zome* (multicolored stripes); the Osaka actor Sanogawa Ichimatsu, who started the fashion for the chessboard pattern (the so-called Ichimatsu pattern) in 1741; and the actors Nakamura Koroku and Nakamura Sen'ya, who made the large tie-dyed designs called *Koroku-zome* and *Sen'ya-zome* popular.

*34. Kosode (one of the* somewake Keicho *kosode). Composite design. About 1600 (Momoyama period). Nagao Art Museum, Tokyo.*

*35. Kosode (Temmon Kosode). Design of tie-dyed* kanoko *spots and embroidered blossoms, leaves, and deer. Second half of sixteenth century (Momoyama period). Tokyo National Museum.*

36. Dofuku *used by Uesugi Kenshin. Patchwork of gold and silver brocades and damask. About 1560 (Muromachi period). Uesugi Shrine, Yamagata Prefecture.*

*37. Kosode. Design of large medallions of wood-sorrel leaves on red figured satin. First half of seventeenth century (early Edo period).*

*38. Kosode. Embroidered and tie-dyed design of chrysanthemums and trellis on white satin. Seventeenth century (early Edo period). Nagao Art Museum, Tokyo.* ▷

*40. Detail of kosode. Design of paulownia leaves and blossoms over a chessboard ground. Seventeenth century (early Edo period). Tokyo National Museum.*

◁ *39. Detail of kosode. Design of flowing water, chrysanthemums, and wisterias. About 1700 (Edo period). Tokyo National Museum. (See also Figure 129.)*

41. *Kosode. Design of willows and characters on green crepe. About 1700 (Edo period).*

42. Furisode. *Design of stream with bush clover on white figured satin. Eighteenth century (Edo period). Nagao Art Museum, Tokyo.* ▷

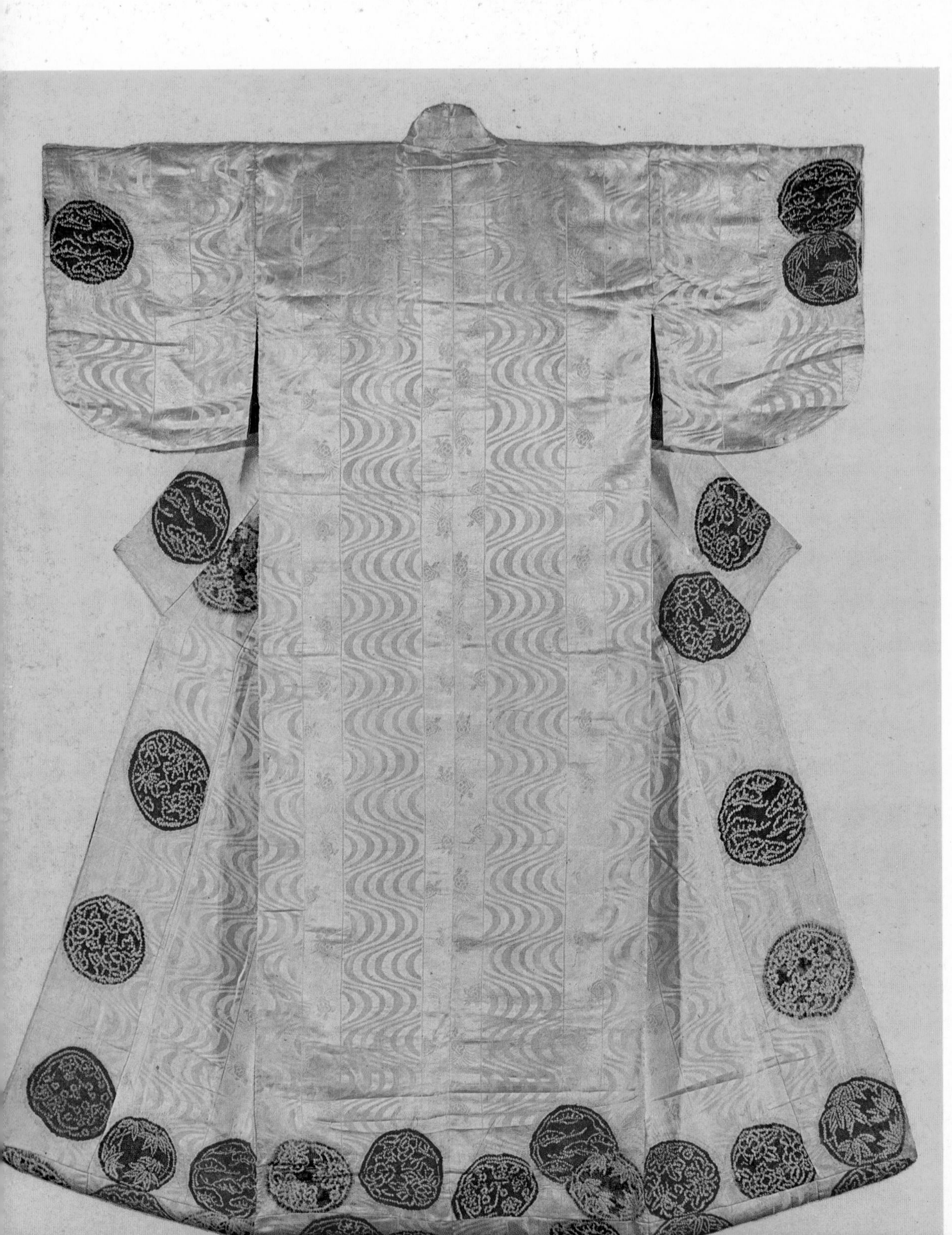

44. *Kosode. Design of arrayed plum sprigs* (yari-ume; *literally, "lance plums"*) *and bamboo on white ground. Second half of seventeenth century (mid-Edo period).*

] 43. *Kosode. Design of scattered medallions on white figured satin. Eighteenth century (second half of the Edo period).*

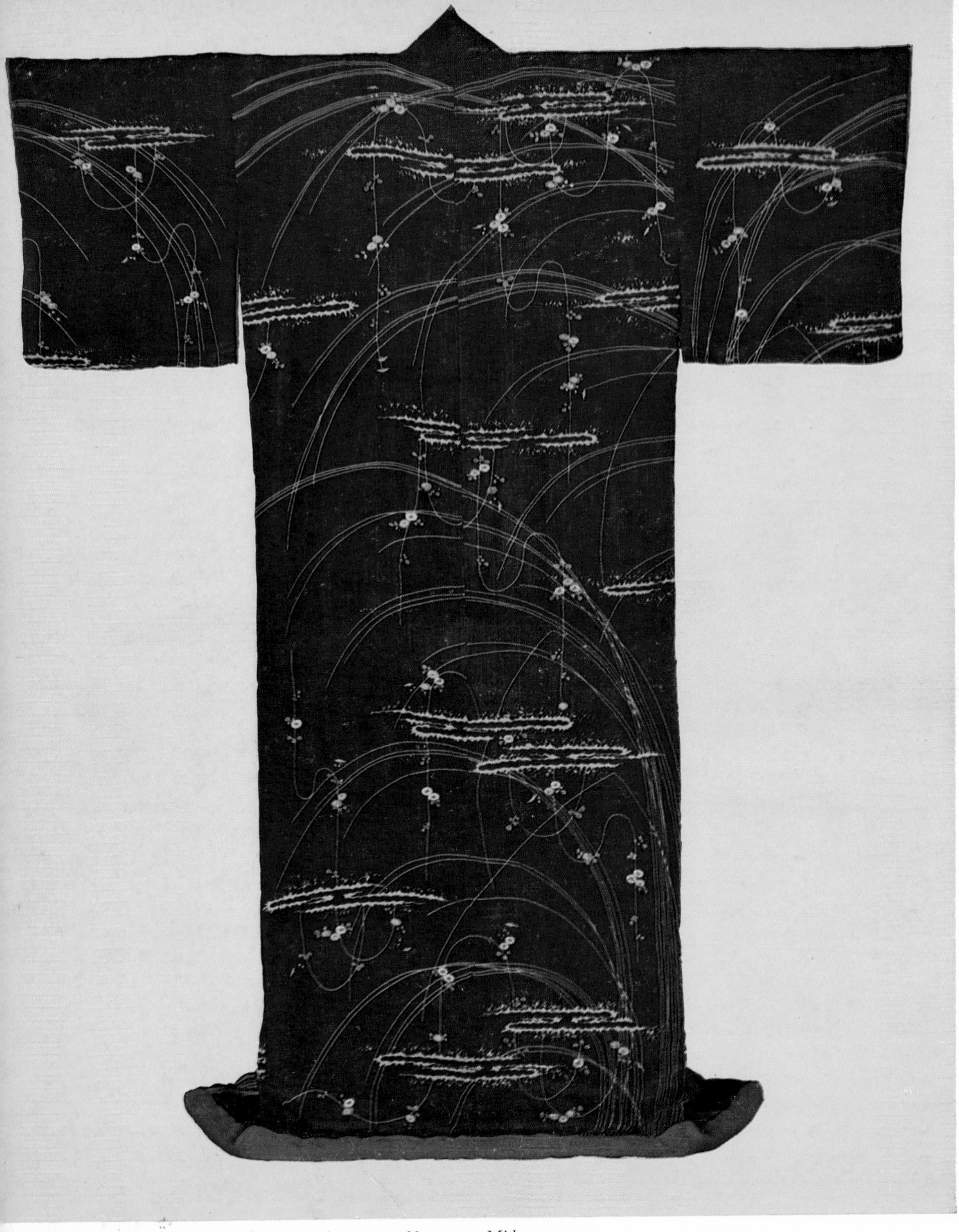

45. *Kosode. Design of vines and chrysanthemums on blue crepe. Mid-eighteenth century (mid-Edo period). Kyoto National Museum.*

CHAPTER THREE

# Noh Costume

JAPAN'S REFINED STAGE ART, the Noh, presents us with a mysterious, graceful beauty in the midst of severity. The performances achieve a heightened effect by combining Noh plays, which are tragic in character and deal with past ages, with Kyogen, comic interludes that deal with subject matter of a timeless kind. Many Noh plays excel in dramatic content and structure, but another factor that heightens their effect is the unique costumes used. They are such an important element that we cannot speak of the beauty of Noh without mentioning them. Costumes so gorgeous that they seem to belong to a different world move about the stage, stylized to the utmost degree. Both costumes and movements are removed from reality and lead the spectator into a world of phantoms. The content of the play is frequently of a melancholy nature, but since the plot often concerns tales of the courts of long-gone reigns, and these sad tales themselves have a phantomlike nature, the effect also has a kind of sweetness.

If the kosode suggests the warmth of the person wearing it, Noh costume suggests a cool, spiritual quality. It has a strange kind of colorfulness. This impression is connected with the mysteriously graceful movements of Noh. The peculiar shapes given to the costumes by the thick, stiff cloths used and the unrealistic poses of the performers are further factors deepening the impression that one is looking at a beautiful world of phantoms (Fig. 47). We see now how important a role costumes play in Noh performances. But were they so important from the start?

SHOGUNAL PATRONAGE Although we are concerned with Noh costume, we must give here a brief account of the origins and development of Noh itself. Noh is said to have reached maturity after the actor-playwrights Kannami Kiyotsugu (1333–84) and his son Zeami Motokiyo (1363–1443) were "discovered" and given patronage by the Ashikaga shogun Yoshimitsu when they were giving a public performance at Ima Kumano in 1374. But Noh had been in existence in provinces like Yamato, Omi, and Ise (modern Nara, Shiga, and Mie prefectures) for a considerable time before that. Its early history is not yet clear, but we do know that perhaps as early as two hundred years before that there were performances in various parts of the country and that companies that were to become the modern Kanze, Hosho, Komparu, and Kongo schools of Noh were active, mainly in the Yamato area. However, as entertainers without official patronage, the Noh performers of those times were poor, and their art was of a low standard, consisting mainly of the kind of mime that would appeal to the common people who were their public. The costumes used at that time must also have been crude. Although Zeami has written much on the performance of Noh, the fact that he says little about costume suggests that not much importance

*46. Noh costume* (happi). *Gift from Ashikaga Yoshimasa. Fifteenth century (Muromachi period). Kanze Collection, Tokyo. (See also Figure 94.)*

was attached to it yet. Early Noh must have presented quite a different aspect from what we know today. The question is, When, why, and how did it come to use the gorgeous costumes so characteristic of it today?

When Noh came under the patronage of the shogun and became the ceremonial musical entertainment of the samurai class, we can presume that Kannami and Zeami provided it with a form suited to its new status. In the perfected form of their art, Noh performers were concerned not only with what they presented but also with the decorum of the presentation. One aspect of this is costume. It seems probable that instead of making new costumes specifically for the stage, the Noh companies received used garments from the shogun's household and wore them for Noh performances.

There was a custom at that time of rewarding a retainer by taking off an item of clothing and presenting it to him. As early as the Heian period, rewards for distinguished service took the form of bolts of cloth, but occasionally a garment that happened to be worn at the time would be presented instead. The recipient would then drape the garment about his shoulders and make his exit. In the case of a dancer, the recipient would perform an encore with the gift in his hands. We know this from picture scrolls and other records of the time. Such scenes were probably common when Noh was performed before the shogun or members of his family in later periods. And these gifts had to be made use of. It is thought that this is how luxurious costumes came to be used for Noh performances. Probably such favors were extended not only to the Kanze school of Noh, founded by

*47. Scene from a performance of the Noh play* Shojo. *The outer robe is a* karaori.

Kannami and Zeami, but also to other schools, and since the use of inferior costumes would be a reflection on a company's dignity, each company must have paid the greatest attention to the costumes it used.

Supporting this view is a costume in the possession of the present head of the Kanze school: the *hitoe-happi* (unlined *happi*) known as the Sempo Hitoe-happi (so called because it was worn only for the Buddhist service called *sempo* in the play *Tomonaga;* Figs. 46, 94). This was a gift from the eighth Ashikaga shogun, Yoshimasa (1436–90), and has a design of a double-*tasuki* (diagonal lattice) pattern and dragonflies distributed within the lattice, both in gold thread on a deep green ground. The design of alternating single and paired dragonflies and the idea of introducing subtle variations by using red, green, yellow, blue, and other colors for the eyes are interesting and typical of Yoshimasa's taste. The *happi* is of a very high technical level, and the design exhibits exceptionl taste—surely a fit garment for Yoshimasa, who was famous for his interest in the arts and anything of refined elegance. I would imagine the *happi* was not brand-new when the Kanze school received it but was, rather, something Yoshimasa was wearing and took off on the spur of the moment to present as a gift. As used in the context of Noh, the word *happi* refers to a garment usually called *ho* in Yoshimasa's time and worn by persons of rank. Since it was an outer robe, it was an easy matter to take it off and bestow it on a retainer. And the fact that it has been so well preserved over the centuries is an indication of the honor the Kanze family felt was attached to this gift.

The *karaori* (literally, "Chinese weave") is an-

*48. Detail from* Kasuga Gongen Kenki Emaki *(Kasuga Gongen Miracles Picture Scroll). 1309. Imperial Household Collection.*

other type of Noh costume in use today. This is a heavy, elaborately patterned brocade garment used for female roles. As the name suggests, it was originally an import from China and far beyond the means of the early Noh performers. The fact that such garments were used suggests that they were gifts from the ladies of the shogun's household.

Behind this growth in elaborateness of Noh costumes was the sense of rivalry felt by the samurai class toward the culture of the court. Since ancient times, the imperial court had had its own ceremonial musical entertainment, *gagaku*. The graceful character of the orchestral and dance pieces in its repertory, many of them deriving from Korean, Chinese, and even Southeast Asian music, made it a fitting embellishment of important occasions. Simply to have adopted *gagaku* as their ceremonial music would have betrayed a lack of resourcefulness on the part of the samurai. And yet, naturally enough, they did want a ceremonial music of their own. They chose Noh as the solution to their dilemma and proceeded to cultivate it as a rival to *gagaku*. Their ungrudging gifts of valuable *karaori* robes were probably motivated partly by such considerations.

As mentioned earlier, many Noh plays are based on tales of the courts of earlier ages, and since the guiding principle of Noh performances at that time was basically one of realism, it followed that performances of such plays had to represent the actual customs and manners of the courts of those times. Knowledge of such customs was easy enough to come by, for contemporary courtiers still maintained the old traditions. Yet in spite of this, the samurai had Noh performed in contemporary costume—in other words, in samurai dress—and one

*49. Noh costume* (nuihaku). *Design of reeds and boats on indigo ground. Seventeenth or eighteenth century (Edo period). Shinshiro Noh Society, Aichi Prefecture.*

50. *Detail of Noh costume* (karaori). Dangawari *design of chrysanthemums and flower baskets. Seventeenth or eighteenth century (Edo period). Shinshiro Noh Society, Aichi Prefecture.*

cannot help sensing here an antagonism toward the court aristocracy. The same rivalry and antagonism lay behind the support and patronage Noh received from Toyotomi Hideyoshi and his family in the Momoyama period and the shoguns and daimyo in the Edo period. The aim of Noh is the creation of a world of phantasms, but if Noh is performed in contemporary dress, then however colorful the costumes may be, the audience is recalled to the world of reality. Thus, since the performers were forced to use contemporary costume, the realistic effect of this had to be countered somehow, and the extreme stylization of movement and gesture may have been one such means.

But from the Momoyama period the situation changed somewhat. Instead of secondhand garments originally worn by their patrons, Noh actors started using costumes made specifically for Noh performances. The term *karaori,* too, no longer referred to imported garments but to costumes made in Japan after the fashion of the original *karaori.* This led naturally to the development of uniquely Japanese designs and techniques and eventually to the birth of costumes peculiar to Noh. Heavy-weave *karaori* was developed for stage effect and was affordable because of the ungrudging patronage of the wealthy daimyo. The use of stiff *karaori* marked another stage in the deepening of the visual beauty of Noh performances.

## TYPES OF NOH COSTUME

The beauty of a Noh performance derives from the simple but strong outlines of heavy-weave costumes like *karaori* (for female roles) and *atsuita* (used principally for male roles). With such thick materials, it is not possible to create a com-

*51. Noh costume* (nuihaku). Katami-gawari *design of clematis scrolls and scattered fans. Seventeenth century (early Edo period). Tokyo National Museum. (See also Figure 65.)*

*52. Noh costume* (karaori). Katami-gawari *design of checks and paulownia leaves with bamboo grass. Second half of sixteenth century (Momoyama period). Amakawa Shrine, Nara.*

plicated, curved outline but only a simple one made up of straight lines and angles, for when the costume is worn, the lines of the body disappear. The stiff, angular effect was suitable for the representation of ghosts and visions. In the case of costumes like the *suikan* and *kariginu,* made from thinner cloths, the weave was deliberately made tight in order to produce a stiff, straight-line silhouette. Thus, although Noh costumes originated in garments worn in ordinary life, they gradually developed in the direction of a stylized beauty.

*Karaori, surihaku, nuihaku,* and *maiginu* are among the costumes used for female roles. Costumes for male roles include *kariginu, choken, mizugoromo, happi, sobatsugi, atsuita, noshime, suo,* and *hangiri.* The *karaori* is used as a woman's outer garment, while the *surihaku* and *nuihaku* are worn as underrobes with the *karaori. Maiginu* literally means "dance robe," and it is in fact used as a woman's dancing costume.

The *kariginu* (Fig. 67) exists in lined and unlined forms. The lined *kariginu* is for roles representing deities and men of high rank, while the unlined version is used for Shinto priests. The *choken* (Fig. 97) is a loose robe resembling the *maiginu* of women's roles and is used for male roles of a rather effeminate nature, such as young noblemen. The *choken* is sometimes used instead of the *maiginu* for female roles because both costumes have a festive, colorful quality. *Happi* (Fig. 71) is the Noh term for what is otherwise known as *ho,* and like the *kariginu,* it exists in lined and unlined versions. The lined *happi* is used for demon gods or generals in battle attire, whereas the unlined version is used for the battle attire of characters like young noblemen. The *sobatsugi* represents armor and is in ef-

*53. Noh costume* (suo). *Design of grasses, flowers, and* shikishi *cards on indigo ground. Second half of sixteenth century (Momoyama period). Kasuga Shrine, Seki, Gifu Prefecture.*

fect a lined *happi* with the sleeves removed. The *atsuita* resembles the *karaori* and is made of heavy brocade with designs in colored, gold, and silver yarns. For demon-god roles, it is worn under garments like *mizugoromo, happi, sobatsugi,* and *choken. Atsuita-karaori* is a costume made from a cloth with a weave resembling *karaori* more closely than ordinary *atsuita.* The *noshime* exists in a plain, unpatterned version and also a version having a design of stripes or checks arranged in horizontal bands. Plain *noshime* were used for old-man and Buddhist-priest roles, while banded *noshime* were used for common people and samurai of low rank. Occasionally, banded *noshime* were also used for lowborn women of mature years. The *suo* (Figs. 53, 74) is an unlined garment of hemp fiber, resembling a simplified version of the *hitatare,* and represents everyday wear of both samurai and commoners. The *hangiri* is a form of *hakama* (trousers) with a rich woven design and is worn with a *happi.* In addition, there are a few special costumes used for Buddhist-priest roles.

These costumes are basically garments commonly worn in Muromachi times, although the names by which they are known in connection with Noh sometimes differ from their common names; thus we can see that practical dress was used as the basis of Noh costume. It is likely that in the early period of the Noh great ingenuity was expended on the choice and adaptation of suitable garments for the various types of roles, just as a limited number of masks were used for all kinds of plays. And

*54. Noh costume* (nuihaku). *Design of snow-laden plantain bush on* dan-gawari *ground. Second half of sixteenth century (Momoyama period). Okayama Art Museum, Okayama Prefecture.*

55. *Noh costume* (nuihaku). Kata-suso *design of flowers and grasses with floral medallions. Second half of sixteenth century (Momoyama period). Okayama Art Museum, Okayama Prefecture.*

*56. Detail of Noh costume* (nuihaku). *Design of reeds and waterfowl. Tokyo National Museum.*

the ways the problems created by such limitations were dealt with gave an added interest to Noh. The use of the *happi* with its stiff outline to suggest a general's armor is a method of symbolic stylization very typical of Noh.

But as Noh gained in popularity, this multiple use of costumes was no longer satisfactory, and differentiation of costumes according to the nature of the role began. Even within the *karaori* group of costumes, which developed from the kosode type of woman's garment, *karaori* including red in their design (*iro-iri*) and having broad, dangling sleeves (*furisode*) were used for young-woman roles, while older-woman roles used a *karaori* with no red in its design (*iro-nashi*). Again, the *kariginu* was originally a garment worn by courtiers, and in order to show its noble character Chinese-style designs and gold brocades were used. This is another example of how shape, coloring, and design were changed according to the social standing of the character for whom the costume was to be used. The *atsuita* was worn under such garments as the *happi, soba-tsugi,* and *choken* in order to emphasize further their strong outlines. The special conventions of Noh performance led to the development of forms of costume peculiar to Noh, and these costumes in turn influenced the conventions of Noh performance. The impression of sculptural bulk that we get from the costumes of female roles is due to the fact that the performers are wearing several layers of heavy-weave material, and although Noh costumes developed from practical garments, this does not mean that the appearance they present to us today is what the nontheatrical garments looked

*57. Noh costume* (noshime). *Design of fine checks in white and blue with brown, blue, red, and yellow stripes. Seventeenth or eighteenth century (Edo period). Tokugawa Art Museum, Nagoya.*

*58. Scene from a performance of the Kyogen* Suo-otoshi.

like in their day. The solemn, deliberate movements of Noh must have developed together with its stiff, bulky costumes.

Along with these changes in the shapes of the costumes, special designs were also developed according to the type of role the costumes were meant for. For example, *karaori* were frequently decorated with patterns of grasses and flowers to emphasize the femininity of a role, or when the role in question was that of a court lady, the design might use some motif related to poetry. Then again, *atsuita* used for "strong" male roles might have large designs of lions, or clouds, or lightning—all symbolizing strength. In the first part of the play *Kurama Tengu,* the *shite,* or principal performer, wears an *atsuita* with a bold check design. This is an example of both the stiff quality of the cloth and its design being used to suggest the strong, rough nature of the role.

## KYOGEN COSTUME

Whereas Noh is tragic in nature, Kyogen is comic. The words of Noh are to a great extent chanted or sung, and dance plays a very important part. In contrast, Kyogen uses a more natural speech delivery, and its movements are more realistic. There are other differences. Noh is basically aristocratic historical drama. Kyogen is contemporary in nature and is a theater of the common people. Kyogen are performed between Noh plays, thereby heightening the tragic character of the Noh plays and at the same time providing comic relief. This contrast between Noh and Kyogen is reflected in costumes.

For the most part, the characters in a Kyogen are neither nobles nor beautiful women—they are usually country bumpkins, simpletons, or the like, and their foolish behavior is the object of laughter. To that extent they create a sense of familiarity in

*59. Kyogen costume* (kataginu). *Design of broken fence and gourd. Eighteenth or nineteenth century (Edo period).*

*60. Kyogen costume* (kataginu). *Design of arrows and targets. Eighteenth or nineteenth century (Edo period).*

the audience. The reason the colloquial language was used in the dialogue of Kyogen was to create such a sense of familiarity, of something close to one's own life. And for the same reason, in contrast with the aristocratic costumes of Noh, Kyogen used the dress of the common people. The history of Kyogen does not seem to have been studied as thoroughly as that of Noh. The plots, the words, and the costumes all date from the Muromachi period. Masks are sometimes used, but usually the face is left uncovered. The costumes are simple. This is probably a vestige of the time when Kyogen performances were improvised, using whatever garments happened to be available. To that extent, Kyogen costume is able to tell us much about the dress of the common people of medieval Japan.

In general, the performer of the role of Tarokaja (head servant) wears a patterned *kataginu* of hemp over a striped *noshime,* with *hakama* trousers decorated with a design of family crests (Fig. 58). On the other hand, the master simply wears a *nagakamishimo* (consisting of a vestlike garment resembling the *kataginu* and a long, trailing *hakama*) over a *dan-noshime* (banded *noshime*).

The most distinctive Kyogen costume is the *kataginu,* decorated with startlingly large designs of such motifs as gourds (Fig. 59) and trivets. These designs seem novel to us today, but there was nothing unusual about them in their time. In the *Kasuga Gongen Miracles* picture scroll (*Kasuga Gongen Kenki Emaki*) of 1309 we can see depictions of low-ranking samurai and servants dressed in clothing with similar large designs. Since these garments were worn by people of low status and since textile

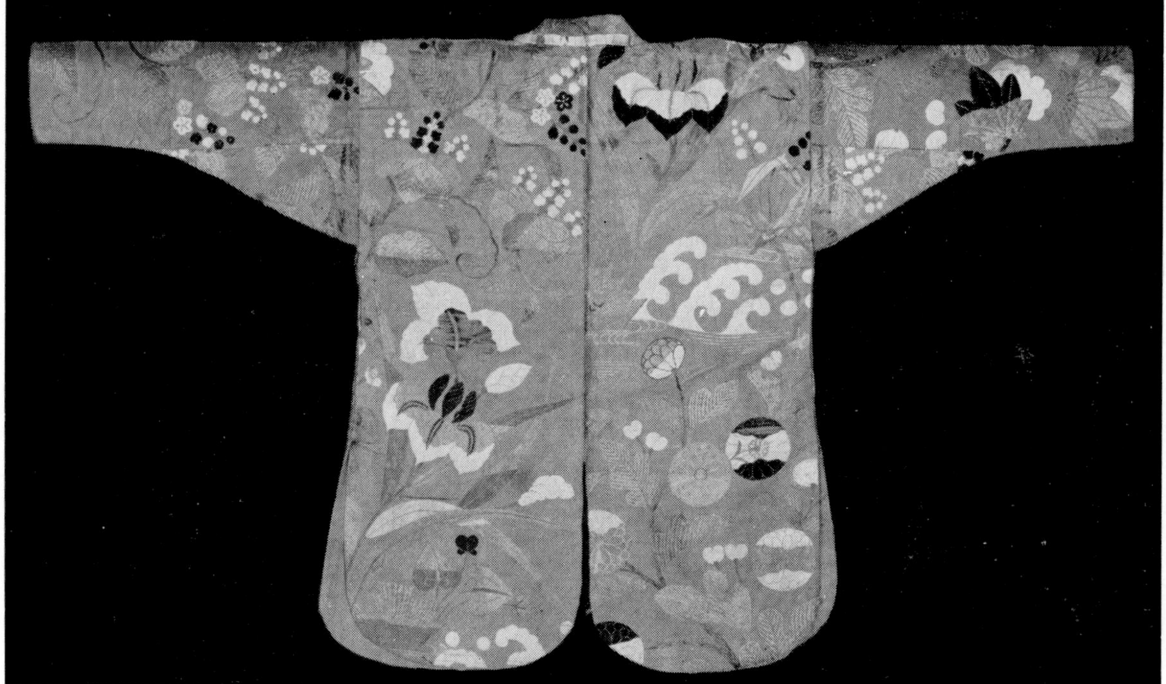

*61. Kyogen costume.* Nuihaku *design of chrysanthemums, lilies, and maple and paulownia leaves. Second half of sixteenth century (Momoyama period). Itsukushima Shrine, Hiroshima Prefecture.*

techniques were not very sophisticated at that time, the designs were probably simple hand-drawn or stencil-dyed designs, like those of the *kataginu* that have come down to us today. The fan-sutra underpainting of Figure 62 shows servants wearing garments with designs produced by these methods, and we may conclude that the common people in general wore clothes with designs executed in these techniques. But, as one might expect of a product of an age when the court was the cultural center of Japan, the fan-sutra paintings show designs using elegant motifs, such as *miru* (a type of edible seaweed) and the comma-shaped *tomoe,* whereas the *Kasuga Gongen Miracles* scroll shows designs of a more rustic taste—cormorants and radishes, for instance. This is not surprising when we remember that this scroll dates from the Kamakura period, when the samurai class ruled the country.

It is interesting that in Kyogen costumes much use is made of simple striped patterns for undergarments (clothing worn under garments like *kataginu* and *hakama*) and *hakama.* Apparently in the Muromachi period striped cloths, being among the simplest types of textiles, were practical materials. The striped patterns are coarse, but with their distinctive color schemes they give the impression of unconventionality that is characteristic of Kyogen. Of course, the garments that have survived from that period are stage costumes, but the feeling that they were similar to garments worn in ordinary life is very strong. Obscured by the sumptuousness of Noh costume, Kyogen costume has not received much attention, but as a reflection of the taste of

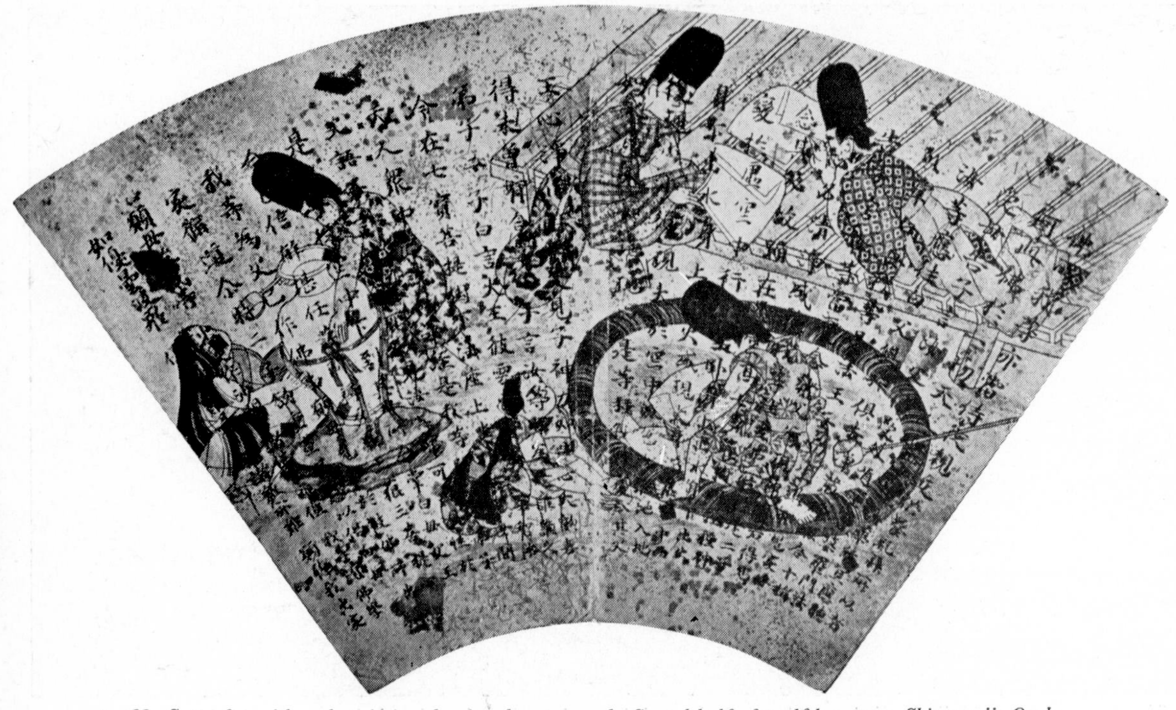

*62. Sutra fan with underpainting showing dyers at work. Second half of twelfth century. Shitenno-ji, Osaka.*

the common people in the middle ages, I think it deserves close study. For in this taste we can detect something of the flavor of the aesthetic ideals of *wabi* (austerity) and *sabi* (refined rusticity), so important in tea-ceremony aesthetics.

A very special kind of costume is used for the Kyogen *Tojin-zumo*. Other Noh and Kyogen costumes are tailored in straight lines and right angles, so to speak, but both the sleeves and the bodies of the *Tojin-zumo* costumes are curved in shape. The impression is that of the exotic dress of a foreign land, and in fact many of these costumes are made from material imported from China. The plot of *Tojin-zumo,* which might be translated as "Wrestling with the Chinese," is as follows. A Japanese in the service of a Chinese king is promised that if he wins a wrestling tournament he will be allowed to return to Japan. After beating nearly fifty wrestlers, he finally wrestles with the king himself and wins. Because the setting of this Kyogen is China, it is only natural that the costumes, too, should have an exotic flavor. But they do point up how the rest of Noh and Kyogen costumes developed into something uniquely Japanese.

For a long time we have lamented a gap in our knowledge of medieval Japanese costume because of the lack of actual examples of garments from this period. But in fact we can see fine examples on the Noh stage, examples that are more artistic than the actual clothes of the time.

*63. Detail of Noh costume* (nuihaku). *Design of hydrangeas and other flowers. Second half of sixteenth century (Momoyama period). Nagao Art Museum, Tokyo.* ▷

*65. Detail of Noh costume* (nuihaku). *Design of scattered fans and clematis scrolls. Seventeenth century (early Edo period). Tokyo National Museum. (See also Figure 51.)*

◁ *64. Noh costume* (nuihaku). *Design of snow-laden willow branches and butterflies. Second half of sixteenth century (Momoyama period). Kasuga Shrine, Seki, Gifu Prefecture.*

*67. Noh costume* (kariginu). *Design of plum trees and butterflies on a yellow ground. 1620. Hakusan Shrine, Gifu Prefecture.*

◁ *66. Kyogen costume. Design of willow branches and herons with gold-leaf mist motifs. Second half of sixteenth century (Momoyama period). Itsukushima Shrine, Hiroshima Prefecture.*

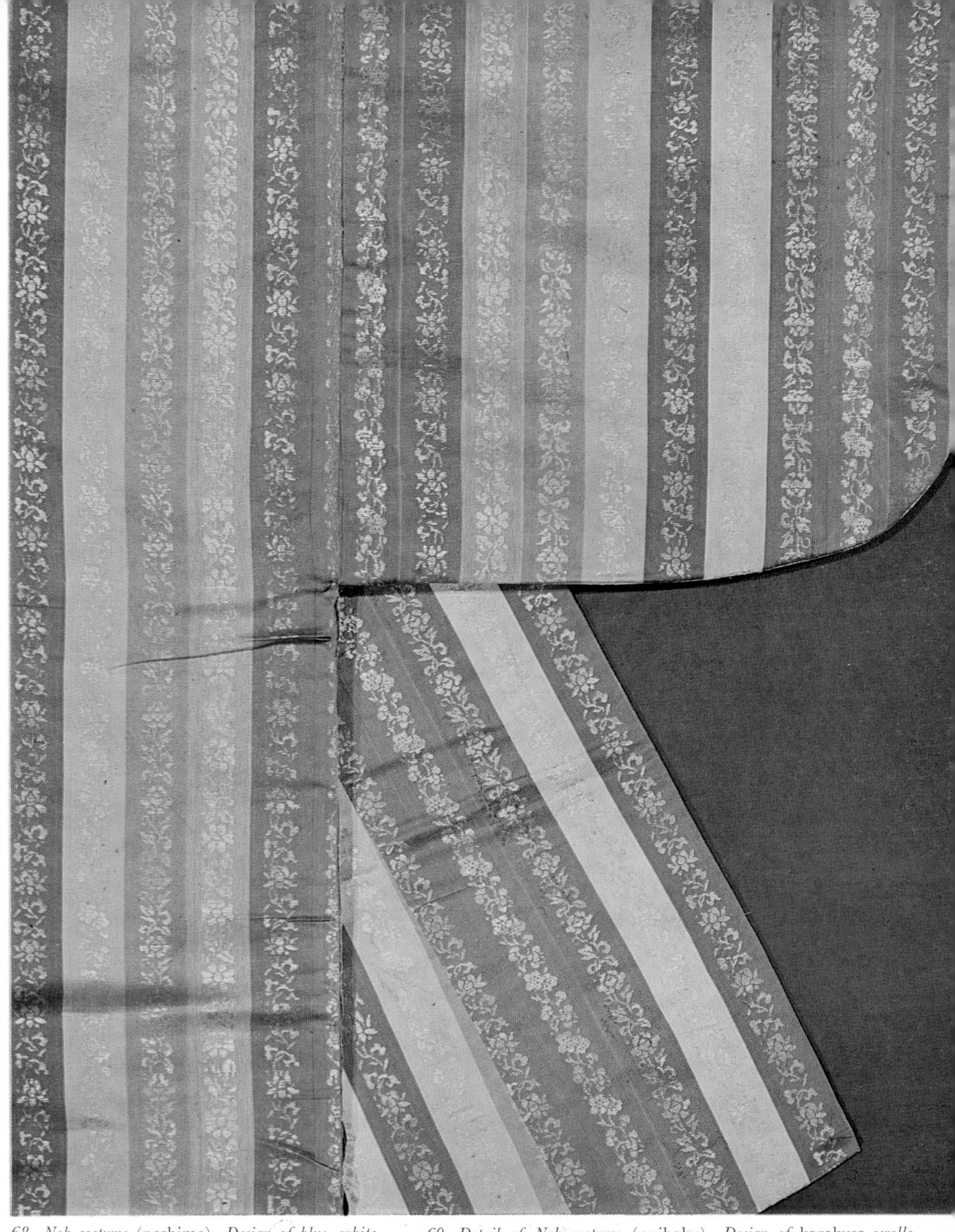

*68. Noh costume* (noshime). *Design of blue, white, red, and green bands. Seventeenth or eighteenth century (Edo period). Tokugawa Art Museum, Nagoya.*

*69. Detail of Noh costume* (nuihaku). *Design of* karakusa *scrolls on multicolored stripes (the so-called Komparu stripes). Seventeenth or eighteenth century (Edo period). Nagao Art Museum, Tokyo.*

*70. Detail of Noh costume* (nuihaku). *Design of ropes and leaves on light blue ground. Seventeenth or eighteenth century (Edo period). Noda Shrine, Yamaguchi Prefecture.*

*71. Detail of Noh costume* (nuihaku). *Design of water in gold leaf with embroidered aquatic plants and baskets. Seventeenth or eighteenth century (Edo pariod).* ▷

*72. Detail of Noh costume* (nuihaku). *Design of scattered square and oblong cards on* dan-gawari *ground design of wisterias. Eighteenth century (Edo period). Tokyo National Museum.*

*73. Noh costume* (nuihaku). Dan-gawari *design of scattered fans and water. Seventeenth or eighteenth century (Edo period).* ▷

*74. Detail of Noh costume* (suo). *Design of* katawa-guruma *(half wheels) and gourds. Eighteenth or nineteenth century (Edo period).*

*75. Detail from folding-screen painting of Kabuki. Seventeenth century.*

## TOWARD KABUKI COSTUME

Just as the subject matter and performance style of Kabuki have been heavily influenced by Noh and Kyogen, so Kabuki costume, too, owes much to the influence of the costumes of these two earlier theater forms. A comparison of the Noh *Ataka* and the Kabuki play *Kanjincho* (The Subscription List), which is based on *Ataka*, will show how similar Noh and Kabuki costumes are. The two types of costume do exhibit, however, the difference between a classical art and a newly risen one, an art enjoying the patronage of the daimyo and one supported by the common people.

Noh and Kyogen had a range of *kata*, or standard gestures and movements, that had developed naturally in the course of innumerable performances over a long period. The newcomer Kabuki, too, used these movements, but they had to be given some kind of novelty. One way of achieving popularity with the masses was to give stage movements a kind of exaggerated realism. At the same time, since the Tokugawa shogunate would not tolerate criticism or the publicizing of embarrassing facts, Kabuki had to disguise its subject matter as fiction. Thus it resorted to devices like setting the action of a play in an earlier age or using obviously unrealistic costumes. How to reconcile the mutually conflicting aims of realism and exaggeration was Kabuki's dilemma. But for the audiences, this unreality had the attraction of allowing them to enjoy themselves for a while in a kind of special world. Unlike Noh costume, which developed out of the needs of Noh performance, Kabuki costume was ex-

*76. Kabuki costume. Design of pine tree and wisterias. Nineteenth century (late Edo period). Tokyo National Museum.*

aggeration for the sake of exaggeration. Its distinctive designs set the fashion for a time, but otherwise it did not influence Japanese dress to any considerable extent.

Noh was privileged in that it enjoyed the patronage of the wealthy daimyo and had at its disposal the most advanced textile techniques for its costumes. For this reason it made a contribution to the development of textile design and techniques in fields other than Noh. Kabuki, on the other hand, rested on the support of the masses, who were by no means wealthy. Thus it was satisfied with external appearance and played no part in the advancement of the textile arts. When we look at examples of Kabuki costumes, we see that they may have served well enough for the stage, but the costumes themselves are of no great artistic value. Figure 76 shows a costume used by the Kabuki actor Bando Mitsue, who had connections with daimyo. But even this, although colorful, has nothing outstanding about it in material or design. Thus, although Noh (including Kyogen) and Kabuki costumes are both types of theatrical costume, they cannot be discussed on equal terms.

CHAPTER FOUR

# The Passage of Time

EARLY KABUKI It was the liberal temper of the Momoyama period that made possible the great leap forward in the development of the kimono. But such freedom is liable to end in exaggeration and artificiality and did in fact lead to a pursuit of the bizarre and exotic. The popularity of the shrine dancer Okuni from the province of Izumo, who danced in male attire, is an example of this phenomenon. Okuni was a beautiful and skillful dancer, but what captured the hearts of her audiences was her dashing appearance on stage dressed as a man. This bizarre performance fitted in with the popular craving for new forms of titillation. But interest in women dressed as men was not confined to this period. The phenomenon has appeared several times in the social history of Japan. The popularity of the *shirabyoshi* (a kind of dance performed by women in male attire) in the late Heian period was similarly due to the fact that a need for some stimulation was felt in the aesthetic life of the time. The beauty recognized in the performance of female roles acted with severe, masculine movements in the Noh is another instance of attraction by the "abnormal," and it excited people's fantasy. The attraction exercised by demon women is also due to a subconscious interest in abnormal feminine beauty. The fad for Okuni Kabuki was by no means due to mere chance.

As if following in Okuni's footsteps, the prostitutes known as bathhouse girls, or *yuna,* appeared on the streets. The painting of bathhouse girls shown in Figure 19 illustrates well their demeanor. Although they are women and are dressed as women, they behave almost as if they were men—sauntering along arrogantly with no sign of modesty. Undoubtedly they conducted themselves in this manner because they knew that men were attracted by it. This tendency is seen again in Kaigetsudo Ando's painting of a courtesan (Fig. 31).

The opposite phenomenon—the feminization of men's dress—also occurred. Good examples of this are the *dofuku* robes worn by Uesugi Kenshin (Fig. 36), Toyotomi Hideyoshi (Fig. 26), and Tokugawa Ieyasu. The pretty, feminine impression one gets from these is the more surprising when one remembers that their owners were military leaders. It is no cause for surprise, then, that the dandies who roamed the pleasure districts were often decked out in such pretty attire as to be mistaken for women. These tendencies presently led to Young Men's Kabuki supplanting Women's Kabuki (Okuni and her successors) in 1629, when the latter was banned. The handsome youths who were the principal performers in Young Men's Kabuki excited the public's curiosity by dressing as women. This too was considered to be an evil influence on public morals and was banned in 1652 after scarcely a quarter of a century.

These currents in the entertainment world were connected with fashions in general. Women's dress gained masculine characteristics, while men's dress

*77. Campaign vest* (jimbaori) *said to have been used by Toyotomi Hideyoshi. Second half of sixteenth century (Momoyama period). Kodai-ji, Kyoto.*

became feminized. The bold patterns of early-Edo kosode and the *tsujigahana* dyed designs so popular for men's kosode (Figs. 33, 78) must both be understood against this background.

EXOTIC TEXTILES The Muromachi and Momoyama periods saw the development not only of Noh costume and the kosode but also of many other typically Japanese arts. Yet at the same time there was a strong infatuation with foreign, exotic things. The shogun's residence and Zen temples of the Muromachi period were decorated with fine hanging scrolls and other rare objects imported from Ming-period (1368–1644) China by shogunate trading missions. This trend represented the new cultural life of the age. Ming products were also copied. The great love for *kinran* and *ginran* (gold and silver brocades, respectively) and damask is a manifestation of the trend. These weaves themselves were unusual, and the designs were also very novel. *Kinran, ginran,* and damask began to be woven in Japan too (in the Nishijin area of Kyoto, for instance), which indicates that the general demand could no longer be satisfied by imports alone.

The arrival of Portuguese ships in the late Muromachi period established contact with Europe and led to the importation of the so-called *namban-mono,* or European goods, even more exotic than Chinese products in Japanese eyes. Imported European products included wool fabrics, gold and silver braid, calico, the so-called *kanto* striped fabrics (Fig. 136), and other articles. The infatuation with *namban-mono* lasted throughout the Momoyama and Edo periods, but in the Momoyama period the sense of novelty was strongest, so that such goods held a particularly strong fascination for the Japanese. Genre paintings of the period frequently show figures dressed in European attire. Other examples of this infatuation include Toyotomi Hideyoshi's colorful *jimbaori* campaign vest (Fig. 77), made from a material resembling Gobelin tapestry weave, and Uesugi Kenshin's cloak of velvet decorated with gold and silver braid. It was natural that such weaves and designs should be imitated, although some time was required for their refinement. *Kanto* and calico fabrics were two of the first to be imitated, and their designs, in particular, were new in Japanese textiles.

It is noteworthy that textiles with very distinctive Japanese characteristics were developed at this time—the time when tie-dyed textiles made their entrance. Tie-dyeing was in fact an old technique, known as far back as the Nara period. Its reentry on the scene in this age when the taste for exoticism was at its peak, and the impression of freshness it gave, were due to the fact that the technique had been refined in the environment of the fashion for exoticism. *Tsujigahana* dyed designs were so popular in the Muromachi and Momoyama periods because of the special effect of their characteristic combination of tie-dyed and hand-painted designs

*78. Quilted kosode used by Tokugawa Ieyasu.* Tsujigahana *dyed design of scattered hollyhock crests. Second half of sixteenth century (Momoyama period). Tokugawa Art Museum, Nagoya.*

79. *Detail of piece of kosode material.* Tsujigahana *dyed design of birds and flowers. Second half of sixteenth century (Momoyama period). Fujita Art Museum, Osaka.*

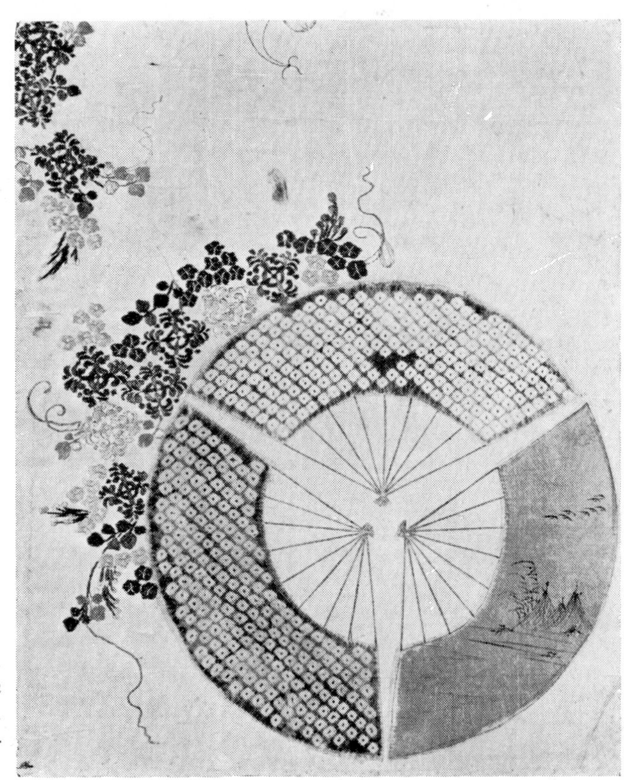

*80. Detail of piece of kosode material. Tie-dyed and embroidered design of fan medallion with vines and small flowers. Second half of sixteenth century (Momoyama period).*

(Figs. 79, 96) resembling those of *kanto* and calico. When I look at *tsujigahana* textiles I am reminded of Furuta Oribe (1544–1615), the famous Christian tea master, for I see a similarity to the shapes and colors of his designs. This coexistence, indeed harmony, of foreign and Japanese styles can be seen in other instances also.

YABO AND IKI Although it is true that the Momoyama period was an age of peace stressing worldly pleasures, this was a temporary peace harboring within it the seeds of the subsequent conflict between Toyotomi Hideyoshi in the west and Tokugawa Ieyasu in the east. People gave themselves up to worldly pleasures because they wanted to enjoy what remained of their lives before the peace came to an end. The tranquility of the Genroku era (1688–1704), in contrast, was the peace of truly stable times. But the pleasures of the Momoyama period, unrestrained to the point of dissipation, had not been forgotten. It is understandable that these embers should catch fire again and create a craving for extravagant beauty. People devoted their energies to outdoing one another in the gorgeousness of their clothes.

A passage in *Muna-zan'yo,* a novel by the Genroku writer Ihara Saikaku, tells us that wealthy women spent vast amounts on elaborately dyed kosode for the New Year's festivities. *Saikaku Oridome,* a collection of writings by the same author, describes how the wife of an Osaka merchant always wore a white kosode as an underkimono, over this a kosode with a tie-dyed design of *kanoko*

*81. Uneme Kabuki. Detail from Kabuki picture scroll. Seventeenth century (early Edo period). Tokugawa Art Museum, Nagoya.*

*82 (opposite page, left). Detail of Noh costume* (karaori). *Design of multiple stripes and floral motifs. Seventeenth or eighteenth century (Edo period). Kongo Collection, Kyoto.* ▷

*83 (opposite page, right). Detail of Noh costume* (atsuita). *Design of checks and flowers on red ground. Seventeenth or eighteenth century (Edo period). Tokugawa Art Museum, Nagoya.* ▷

spots, and finally an outer robe of finely woven black *habutae* silk with a design of "wisteria and wheel" crests at the hem. Around her waist she wore an elaborately dyed obi of *shusu* satin. Both passages note how the commoners' dress had rapidly grown increasingly luxurious. It was natural that the merchants, with their wealth, should have competed among themselves in the beauty of their clothing. Various interesting episodes in this rivalry are recorded.

One day in the Genroku era the womenfolk of wealthy merchants of Edo, Osaka, and Kyoto held a costume competition in the Higashiyama area on the eastern outskirts of Kyoto. The wife of Naniwaya Juemon of Osaka wore a robe of scarlet *rinzu* (figured satin) with famous scenic spots of Kyoto embroidered on it in silver and gold. The wife of Ishikawa Rokubei of Edo wore a kosode with a design of scattered *nanten* (*Nandina domestica*) berries made from coral. The wife of Nakamura Kuranosuke of Kyoto wore a kosode of black *habutae* (fine, smooth silk) over a completely white undergown. Her obi was of antique imported gold brocade. This noble, dignified dress, we are told, overwhelmed the other women. The designer is supposed to have been the famous artist Ogata Korin (1658–1716), who was a friend of the Nakamura family.

Datè Tsunamune, daimyo of the fief of Sendai, used to visit the courtesan Takao in a conspicuously showy outfit. It throws an interesting light on the character of the Genroku era that he was

responsible for a veritable wave of dandyism throughout Edo, so much so that *datè* came to mean "dandyism." The licensed quarters and the theater were the breeding grounds of this dandyism.

However, this unbridled extravagance could not be permitted for long. The shogunate issued one sumptuary edict after another. The champions of *iki* (perhaps best translated as "chic") made some attempts to resist this suppression. The resistance was at the same time a violent reaction to *yabo*, a term used to contrast with *iki* and meaning something like "uncouth, out of date."

Interest in *iki*, the "chic" taste that developed in the Edo period, has waned, but it is one outstanding form of refined beauty bequeathed to us from the Edo period. On investigation we find that it originated as a reaction to the trite taste known as *yabo* that was common at that time. The freedom of dress enjoyed by men and women, young and old, in the Momoyama period was like a myriad flowers blooming simultaneously. During its swift rise, this newly gained freedom brought in its wake rich creative activity. As time went on, however, creativity weakened, and what was left was repetition and reduplication of stereotyped forms. This triteness of design and technique was labeled *yabo*.

Among the factors that helped to develop *yabo* taste were the so-called *gosho* (palace) style and *goshuden* (samurai) style. Though costumes with startling designs were common even among the daimyo at that time, the imperial court of the Momoyama period avoided anything outlandish.

*84. Kosode. Pale purple crepe; design of plum tree and round windows. Seventeenth century (early Edo period). Nagao Art Museum, Tokyo.*

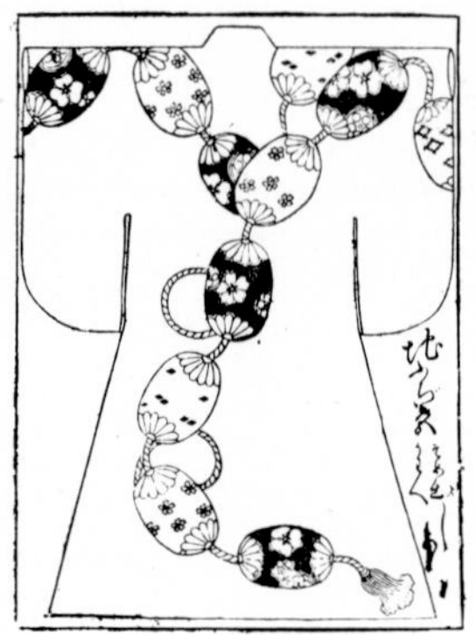

*85. Two pages from a kosode design book* (Kosode On-hiinagata). *1677.*

It may be that the courtiers felt scandalized by the opulent beauty of the outside world and considered it the ostentation of parvenus. Within the imperial palace, use of restrained patterns called *yusoku* was a long-standing tradition. And at the beginning of the Edo period, designs consisting of many small motifs, called *gosho-zome,* or "palace dyed designs," were developed. These are the designs now known as *gosho-toki.* Cloth with these designs is said to have been made sometime between 1624 and 1644 on the instructions of the cloistered dowager empress and sent to various people as gifts. The designs, it is true, were new, but the striving after "good taste" meant that they were unable to escape the charge of being *yabo,* or "old hat."

The influence of the *gosho-toki* designs extended to the shogunal ladies' apartments and the households of the daimyo. By this point in the Edo period, the ruling class had forsaken their hitherto free and easy ways and were striving to maintain the dignified behavior that befitted their station. As a result the daimyo began to imitate the *gosho* style, creating the so-called *goshuden* style. It is not surprising, then, that *yabo* "good taste" persisted. But there appears to have been some resistance to *yabo* even within the ladies' apartments of the shogun's palace. We have the *furisode* (Fig. 107) of Keisho-in, a concubine of the third Tokugawa shogun, Iemitsu (r. 1623–51). It has a bold design of a plum tree extending from the shoulders to the hem that clearly exhibits the sensibility of the new age. Such a development does not seem strange

*86. Page from kimono design book* (Hiinagata Michikaze). *1745.*

*87. Kosode (Korin Kosode). Design of autumn plants on white ground, hand-painted by Ogata Korin. About 1700 (mid-Edo period). Tokyo National Museum.*

when we remember that beautiful townswomen were wielding power in the ladies' apartments.

## SIMPLIFICATION AND REFINEMENT

The aesthetic of *iki,* which pursued the ideals of simplicity and refinement, was born as a reaction to *yabo.* What the followers of this aesthetic were aiming at was to eliminate as much as possible of the superfluous and to manifest beauty in what remained. The word *iki* is written with a character meaning "pure, unadulterated." An example of *iki* taste was the suppression of bright colors in favor of more delicate ones. Another manifestation was the tendency to avoid the open display of expensive decoration but to lavish money on some unobtrusive detail.

There is a story that once when Toyotomi Hideyoshi visited the famous tea master Sen no Rikyu (1522–91) in order to view his morning-glories, Rikyu had all the morning-glories in the garden removed and put a single blossom in a vase in the tokonoma alcove of the tearoom. This attitude is representative of *iki,* and the so-called Korin kosode (Figs. 5, 87) exemplifies it. The design of this kosode was painted by Ogata Korin for a lady of the Fuyuki family, who were wealthy timber merchants in the Fukagawa area of Edo. The beauty of the garment stems partly from Korin's delicate brushwork. But at the same time the idea of having pale-colored autumn plants painted against a plain white ground, in an age when all were vying in the opulence of their clothes, is an

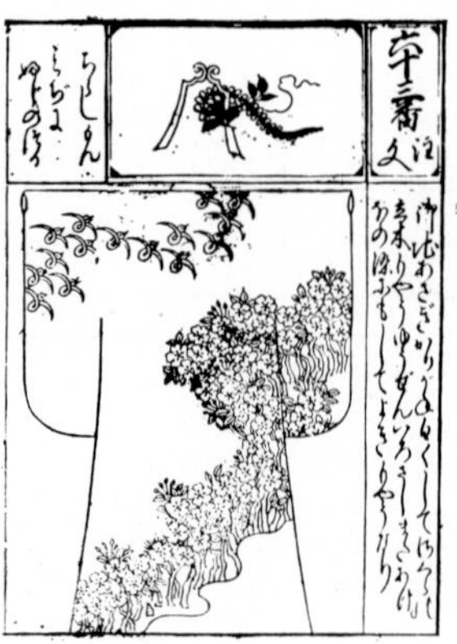

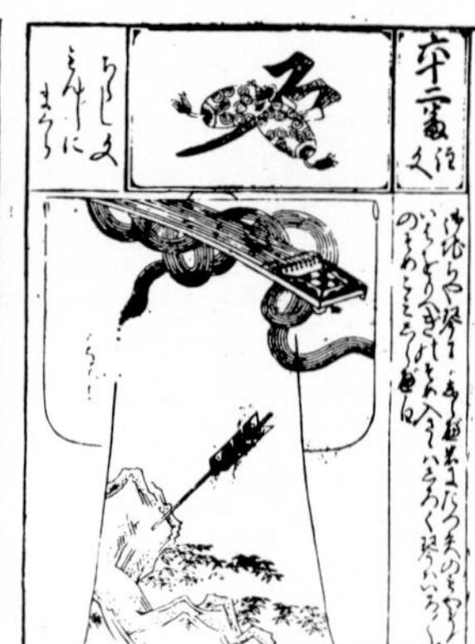

excellent example of the spirit of *iki*. The design seems rather simple for a garment to adorn a lady of a rich merchant family, but the idea of commissioning Korin, who was at the height of his popularity, to execute it was brilliant—the very essence of *iki*. Korin understood what was wanted and took pains to keep his touch light and delicate.

The design of the kosode shown in Figure 106 is basically no more than a simple line-design in red on a red-and-white *kanoko* allover tie-dyed ground, but the *kanoko* spots are perfectly aligned. The color combination alone is perhaps not especially impressive, but a careful look will show that the ultimate techniques of a master dyer's art have been lavished on the robe.

In the second half of the Edo period the *iki* aesthetic showed new developments. When extravagant clothes were prohibited by a sumptuary edict, people tried, in reaction to the laws, to have some bright touch on their clothes in an inconspicuous place. Wearing a colorful underkimono under a plain outer robe was the Edo sophisticate's style. In the simplicity and refinement of *iki* there had to be a spirit of rebellion against authority and established ideas. For example, the reason young women deliberately avoided bright colors and chose clothing of subdued colors was that they knew that they thereby gained the attraction of the unexpected. On the other hand, the fact that the beauty of *iki* was so highly praised is an indication of how widespread *yabo* taste must have been. *Iki,* as a rebellion against the prevalent *yabo* taste, has given us a penetrating insight into the history of Japanese costume.

◁ *88 (opposite page, left). Kosode. Design of mandarin ducks and waves. Seventeenth century (early Edo period). Tokyo National Museum.*

◁ *89 (opposite page, right). Two pages from kosode design book* (Waguni Hiinagata Taizen). *1698.*

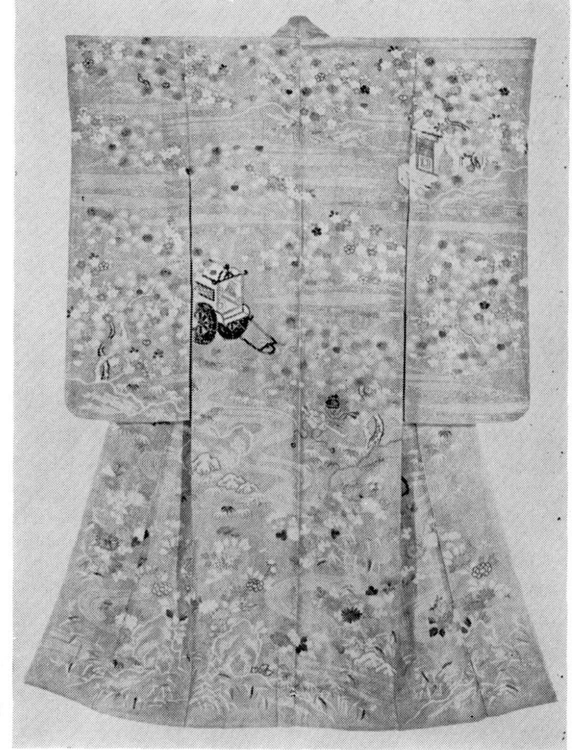

*90.* Furisode. *Light-blue gauze;* yuzen *dyed design of the type called* gosho-toki. *Eighteenth or nineteenth century (late Edo period).*

Extant examples of both Noh costume and kosode from around the Momoyama period are of outstanding quality. Their designs excel not only in color combinations but also in composition, and the conception of the forms exhibits an unusual degree of technical mastery. Noh costumes and kosode cannot be made by craftsmen alone. There must also be artists who draft the designs to be used. But the historians of Japanese textiles have completely ignored their existence. A woodblock print is created through the cooperation of designer, engraver, and printer, but in the last analysis it is the designer who gives the print its value. Sharaku and Utamaro are famous, but the names of their engravers and printers are not much mentioned. In the textile field the same kind of cooperation is involved, but the designer, who should be the most important member of the collaboration, is ignored. And the fact that design and painting skill are involved is given only scant attention. But when we examine the depiction of individual flowers and grasses, although the processes of dyeing or weaving have distorted the character of the original design to a considerable extent, we can still recognize that no mean skill was required.

Up to now, historians of Japanese painting have not dealt with this type of designer-artist. But that any number of excellent designers did exist is shown quite clearly by the many fine costumes extant. I would now like to give a little attention to these unrecognized and unrewarded designers.

First, I want to show that the designs were genuine paintings of considerable artistic value. One example is the *surihaku* Noh costume with a design

91. *Noh costume* (surihaku). *Design of grapes and* shikishi *squares in gold leaf on a purple ground. Second half of sixteenth century (Momoyama period). Tokyo National Museum.*

92. Furisode. *Allover tie-dyed design of clouds and bamboo. Seventeenth century (early Edo period). Tokyo National Museum.* ▷

in gold-leaf appliqué of grapes and *shikishi* (squarish shapes), inside which additional motifs appear (Figs. 91, 97). The grapes are represented very accurately, and the vines exhibit great vitality and freshness. This design is on an artistic level that does not suffer by comparison with extant paintings from the Momoyama period. Next we have the *nuihaku* Noh costume with a design in gold leaf and embroidery of pines and butterfly medallions (Fig. 93). In the varied forms of the butterflies we recognize something out of the ordinary, and in the vigorous form of the pine we feel something of the power of the large picture areas of folding screens. Another *nuihaku* (Fig. 114) has a design of courtiers' carriages and lilies. The lilies are shown the same size as the carriages, but surprisingly enough, these unnatural proportions make the stylized design more effective. What we have here is not merely a mastery of painting technique but also a rich sense of design. What kind of painter was able to produce these designs?

The first possibility is that they were done by the painters patronized by the shogunate. Nowadays people tend to think of these *goyo-eshi* (official painters) as being concerned only with pure, "art" paintings, but in fact their duties also included decorating furniture and buildings. This tradition was an old one dating back to the official painting bureaus of the Nara and Heian periods, and even the painters of the Kano school in the Edo period produced many designs for the shogunate. Kano Motonobu (1476–1559), who became *goyo-eshi* to the Ashikaga shogunate, learned the Tosa style in addition to his own *kanga* style, and this was because it was his duty as *goyo-eshi* to absorb a variety of painting styles. Another good example is Motonobu's grandson, Eitoku (1543–90), who made a design for a lacquered saddle (Figs.

*93. Detail of Noh costume* (nuihaku)*. Design of pines, wisterias, and butterflies. Second half of sixteenth century (Momoyama period). Kasuga Shrine, Seki, Gifu Prefecture.*

*94 (top). Detail of Noh costume (unlined* happi; *gift from Ashikaga Yoshimasa). Fifteenth century (Muromachi period). Kanze Collection, Tokyo. (See also Figure 46.)* ▷

*95 (bottom). Noh costume* (choken). *Gauze; design of weeping-willow branches and swallows. Eighteenth or nineteenth century (Edo period). Uomachi Noh Society, Toyohashi, Aichi Prefecture.* ▷

115, 116). We can surmise that the ruling class of the Momoyama period had well-known painters design their clothes. This period saw a new departure in the decorative paintings on sliding partitions and folding screens, as well as the excellent designs of Noh costumes and kosode. The reason for the quality of the latter is not only that they were products of the same age as the paintings. It probably also lies in the fact that there were close connections between the painters of the screens and partitions and the designers of the costumes. The painters of the time were versatile enough to manage not only large paintings but also designs for applied arts, such as costumes.

However, it was not possible for a small number of painters to satisfy the swiftly growing demand for designs from the common people. It was only natural that drapery merchants started training their own resident designers. The rise of outstanding artists like Ogata Korin and his potter brother Ogata Kenzan (1663–1743) from the family of the drapery merchants Kariganeya, suppliers to Empress Tofukumon-in, is probably due to the fact they had many designers around them. Although the seventeenth-century decorative painter Tawaraya Sotatsu is thought to have been a fan painter originally, the theory has been put forward recently that he had a textile-design background. This is interesting, for the grapevines on the *surihaku* Noh costume of Figure 97 resemble the vines on a lac-

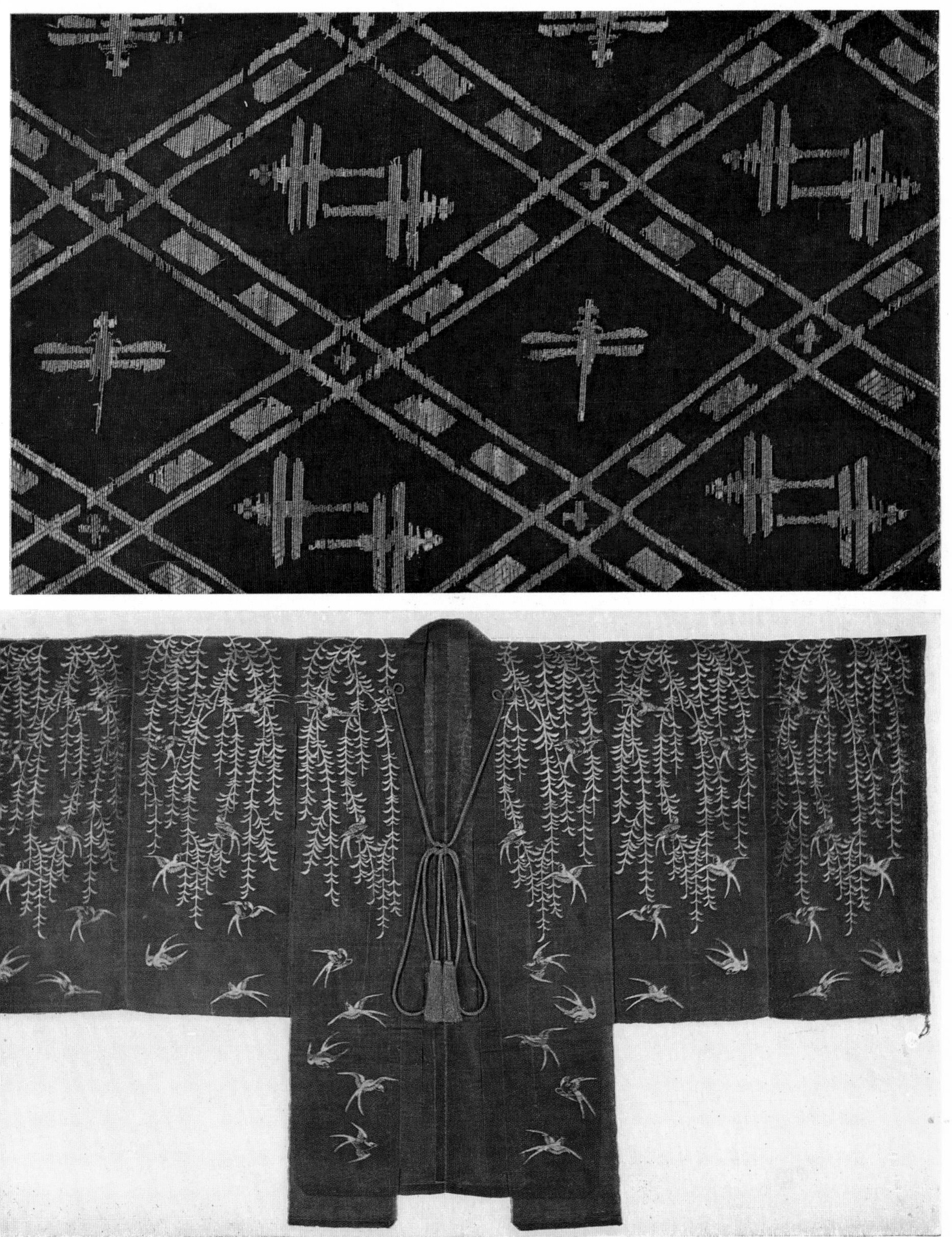

96. *Detail of kosode material.* Tsujigahana *design of flowering plants and chessboard checks. Second half of sixteenth century (Momoyama period).*

97. *Detail of Noh costume* (surihaku). *Design of grapes and* shikishi *squares in gold leaf on purple ground. Second half of sixteenth century (Momoyama period). Tokyo National Museum.*

*98. Noh costume* (nuihaku). *Design of willows over basketwork pattern. Second half of sixteenth century (Momoyama period). Nagao Art Museum, Tokyo.*

*99. Detail of Noh costume* (nuihaku). *Design of windmills on banded ground. Eighteenth or nineteenth century (Edo period). Noda Shrine, Yamaguchi Prefecture.*

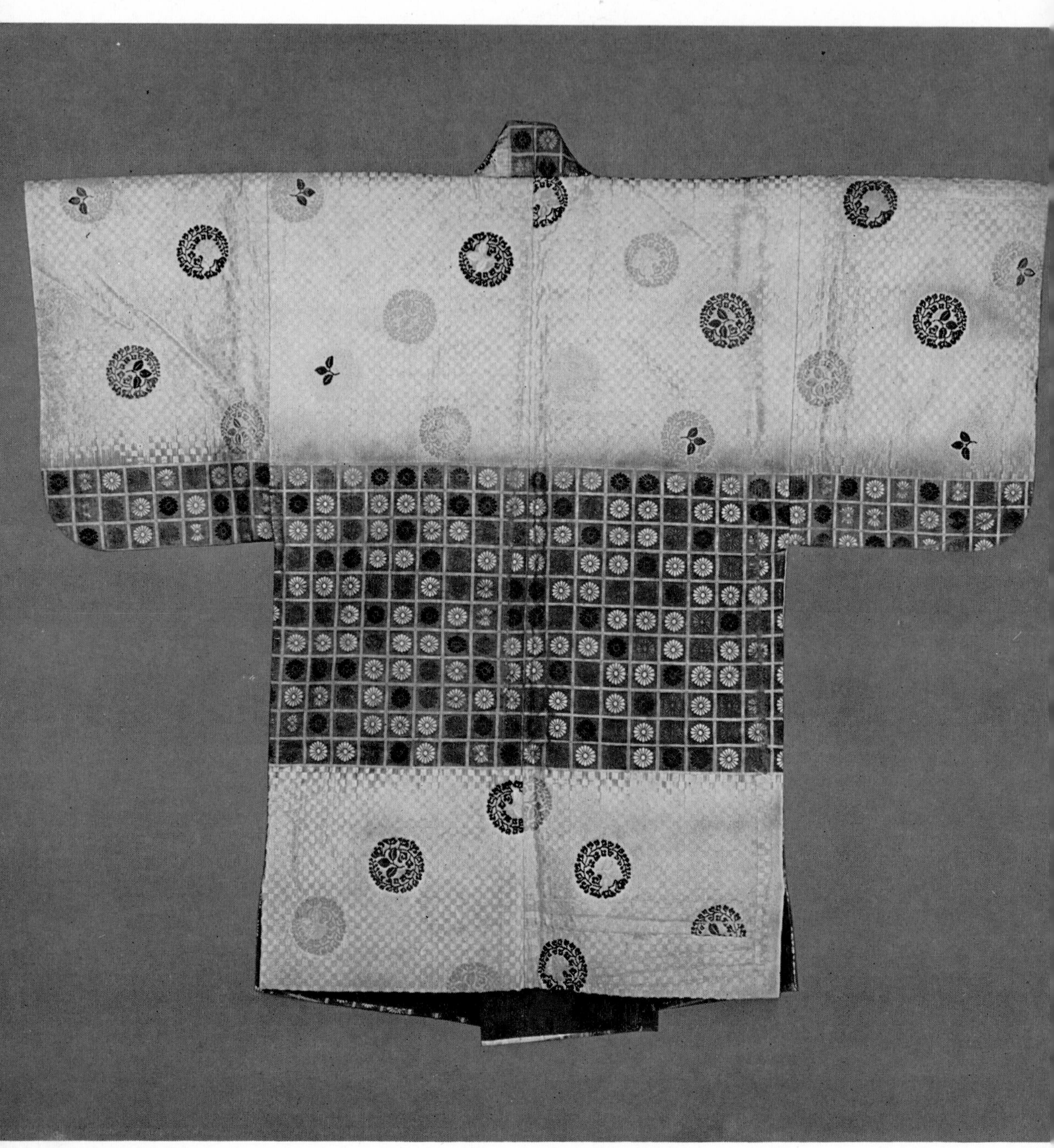

*100. Noh costume* (atsuita). *Design of wisteria medallions and chrysanthemums on banded ground of chessboard checks and trellis. Seventeenth or eighteenth century (Edo period). Itsukushima Shrine, Hiroshima Prefecture.*

*101. Kosode. Figured satin; composite* nuihaku *design of flowers and trees. Late sixteenth century (Momoyama period).*

*102. Detail of Noh costume* (atsuita). Dan-gawari *check design. Seventeenth or eighteenth century (Edo period). Noda Shrine, Yamaguchi Prefecture.*

*103. Detail of Noh costume* (nuihaku). *Design of hydrangeas. Seventeenth century (early Edo period). Suntory Art Museum, Tokyo.*

*104. Detail of Noh costume* (atsuita). Dan-gawari *check design. Seventeenth or eighteenth century (Edo period). (See also Figure 119.)*

*105. Detail of Noh costume* (karaori). *Design of chrysanthemum medallions and crane lozenges. Seventeenth or eighteenth century (Edo period). Itsukushima Shrine, Hiroshima Prefecture.*

◁ *106. Kosode. Tie-dyed design of snow-laden bamboo grass and cherry blossoms in red on red-and-white* kanoko *ground. Second half of seventeenth century (early Edo period). Tokyo National Museum.*

*107.* Furisode *used by Tokugawa Iemitsu's concubine Keisho-in. Design of plum tree on black ground. Late seventeenth century (mid-Edo period). Gokoku-ji, Tokyo.*

*109. Kosode.* Surihaku *design of floral lozenges on shoulders and sleeves and embroidery design of bush clover at hem, both on black figured satin. Second half of seventeenth century (early Edo period). Nagao Art Museum, Tokyo.*

◁ *108. Kosode.* Yuzen *dyed design of chessboard checks, falcons, maples, and waterfalls, with embroidered characters on back and sleeves. Late seventeenth century (mid-Edo period). Nagao Art Museum, Tokyo.*

*110. Kosode. Design of square and oblong cards with flowers and grasses on black figured satin. Eighteenth century (mid-Edo period). Nagao Art Museum, Tokyo.*

*111. Detail of* katabira *summer kimono.* Chaya-zome *dyed landscape. Eighteenth century (Edo period). Ohiko Textile Art Research Institute, Tokyo.*

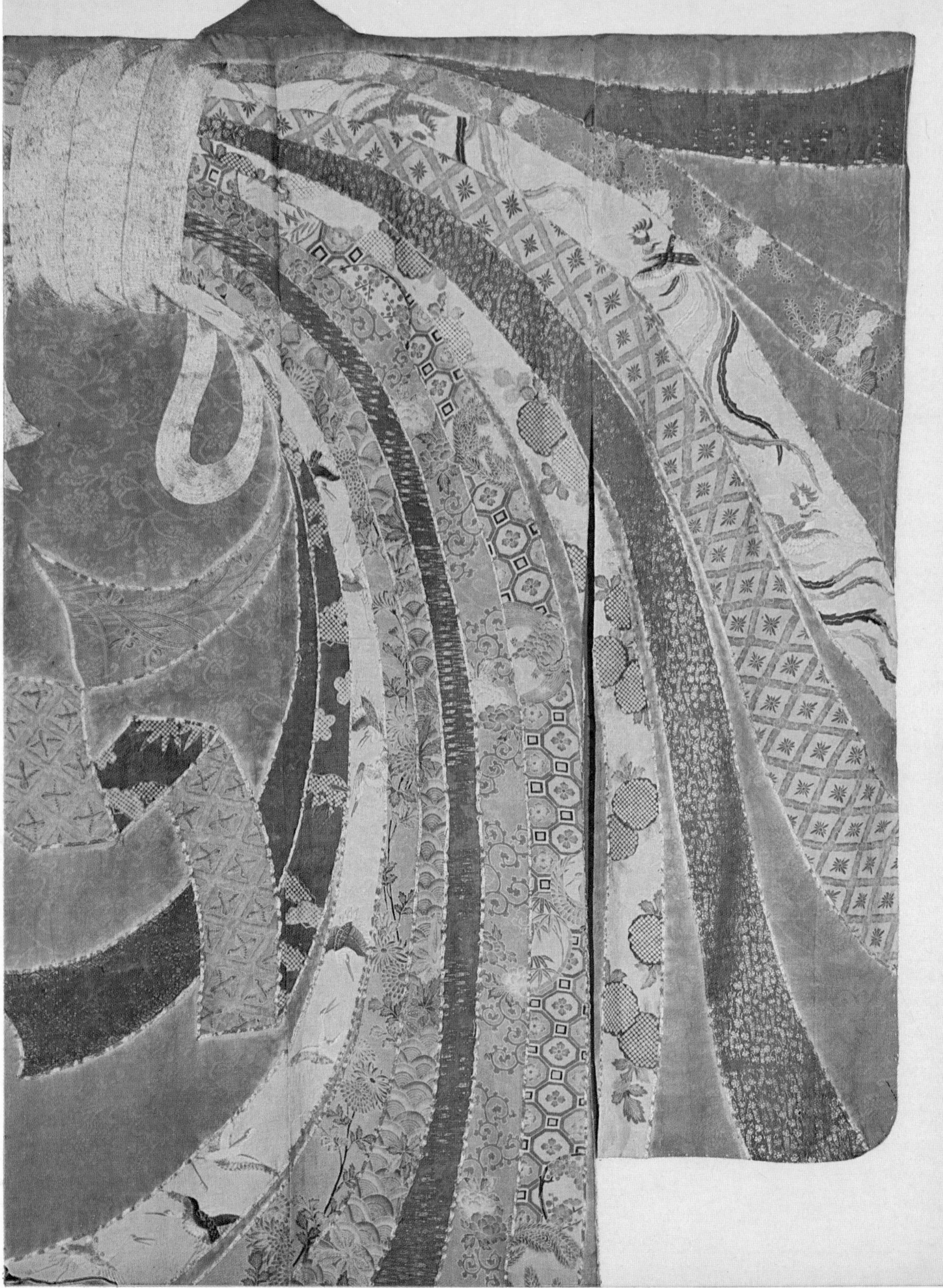

◁ *112. Detail of* furisode. Yuzen *dyed design of stylized bundle of* noshi *(dried strips of abalone, considered auspicious) on red figured satin. Seventeenth or eighteenth century (mid-Edo period). Yuzen History Society, Kyoto.*

*113. Kosode. Pale yellow crepe; design representing the "Eight Scenic Spots of Omi." Eighteenth century (mid-Edo period). Nagao Art Museum, Tokyo.*

*114. Detail of Noh costume* (nuihaku). *Lilies and courtiers' carriages. Second half of sixteenth century (Momoyama period). Tokyo National Museum.*

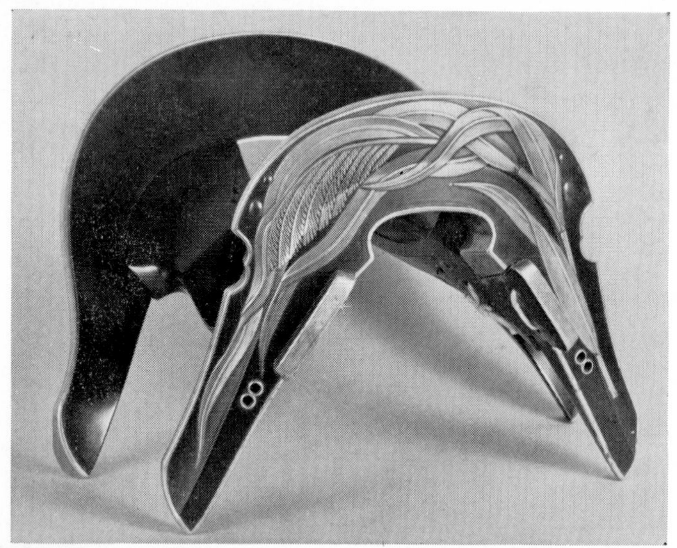

*115. Lacquerware saddle with reed design in* maki-e. *Second half of sixteenth century (Momoyama period). Tokyo National Museum.*

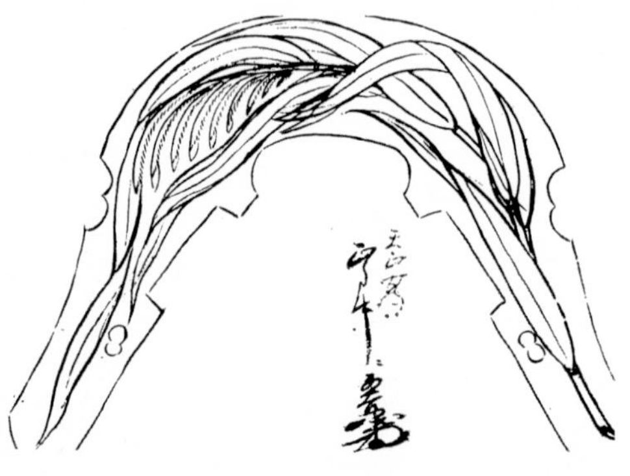

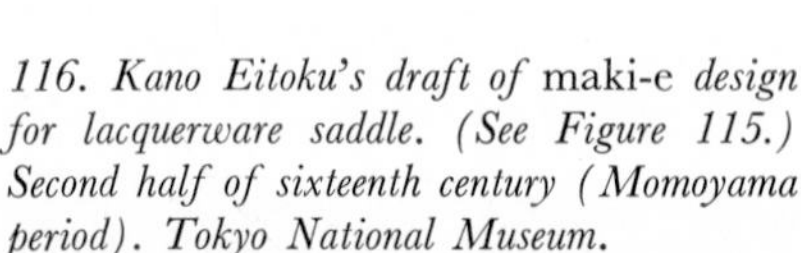

*116. Kano Eitoku's draft of* maki-e *design for lacquerware saddle. (See Figure 115.) Second half of sixteenth century (Momoyama period). Tokyo National Museum.*

*117. Lacquerware chest with* maki-e *design of vines. Sixteenth century. Itsukushima Shrine, Hiroshima Prefecture.*

quered box thought to have been designed by Sotatsu (Fig. 117). It is difficult to state categorically that the resemblance is purely coincidental.

Although there were cases of decorative designers developing into painters in the full sense of the word, the majority remained designers to the ends of their lives, unrecognized and unrewarded. But their design abilities were polished daily in their utilitarian work, and it is due to them that so many fine textile designs are to be seen in costumes from the early Edo period. Although they did not have high social standing, they did have the perseverance and creativity of painters.

However, by the middle of the Edo period, creativity had waned, and designers had become mere craftsmen either copying or reshuffling earlier designs. We know this because among extant garments from this time there are none that are outstanding as examples either of design or of painting. In the Meiji era (1868–1912), the textile manufacturers of the Nishijin area in Kyoto, which was the center of textile manufacture in Japan, commissioned famous painters to create designs for them in an effort to improve the vulgarized designs of the time. Although these artists of the Maruyama and Shijo schools could produce respectable paintings, they had received no design training, and the touch of realism that they added to the designs in fact merely vulgarized them further. When we consider this, our appreciation of the fine garments that have survived from the Momoyama and early Edo periods, when painting and design were inseparable, grows all the stronger.

CHAPTER FIVE

# Changing Tastes

## KATAMI-GAWARI AND KATA-SUSO

Noh costume and the kosode are both developments in Japan's tradition of costume art. I would like to consider now the composition of the designs of this tradition from various points of view. *Katami-gawari* (literally, "half the body different"; Figs. 51, 52, 118, 131) is a type of design in which the right and left halves of the garment are made from different cloths, or at least are of different patterns or colors. This is a device often seen in *karaori* Noh costumes, and its simple, bold conception is extremely satisfying. Although it is an apt symbol of the heroic character of the Momoyama period, the *katami-gawari* was no innovation of this period but had existed from earlier times.

In the fourteenth-century *Kasuga Gongen Miracles* picture scroll we see a man of low station wearing a garment with different colors and patterns on the left and right sides (Fig. 121). This is not a particularly fancy costume, and since it is worn by a servant, it cannot have been especially costly. Let us look at some of the factors that led to the rise of this kind of design.

It is natural for people to wish for change and variety in their clothing. But the pursuit of variety has both financial and technical limitations. One solution to this problem in the past was to take two completely different kimono, cut them both in half, and join the left half of one to the right half of the other and vice versa, thus creating two new garments. This was also a useful way of making use of the good parts of a kimono when a part of it had been soiled or damaged. The *katami-gawari* garment of the servant in the *Kasuga Gongen Miracles* scroll probably had this kind of practical consideration behind it.

There is something refreshing about a design clearly divided in two, and the device was appreciated for aesthetic as well as practical reasons. This kind of design goes back to the Nara and Heian periods in the form of the joined *shikishi* (cards of squarish format) used to write poems on. From the Nara period we have a manuscript of the *Yueh I Lun* (in Japanese, *Gakkiron*) preserved in the Shoso-in repository in Nara, and from the Heian period we have a copy of the *Kokin-shu* (the first imperial anthology of poetry, completed in 905). In both cases variety was achieved by joining together pieces of paper of different colors. An extension of this method can be seen in the paper used for the *Sanjuroku-nin Kashu* anthology (Fig. 120) in the Nishi Hongan-ji temple in Kyoto. Here papers of different colors and designs are joined together in endless variations: cut-and-joined, torn-and-joined, overlapping. By this means, from a few basic types of paper many different designs can be created. It was an ingenious method of increasing the number of different designs. In the same way that the joined *shikishi* were the result of necessity, the idea of *katami-gawari* grew out of practical considerations.

However, since the *katami-gawari* designs of the

*118. Noh costume* (karaori). Katami-gawari *design of checks and grapes with* karahana *stylized-flower motifs. Second half of sixteenth century (Momoyama period). Katte Shrine, Nara.*

Momoyama period were used on costumes of great luxury, they must have been used for their value as design rather than as an economy measure. In an attempt to make designs more complex, two garments were combined into one, so to speak. Even among old examples, there are some pioneering garments that transformed the formerly lowly *katami-gawari* into a noble thing of great value. This is a manifestation of the bold quality of that age.

Once the *katami-gawari,* divided vertically into two, was accepted, a variation using a horizontal division was born, and subsequently the two were combined to result in a kind of chessboard pattern. This is known as *dan-gawari* (literally, "stepwise different"; Figs. 9, 13, 73, 119). The design is even more colorful than the *katami-gawari* and was much used for Noh costumes. These combinations were used purely for aesthetic reasons, economic considerations playing no part. Very often *dan-gawari* designs were made not by joining together different cloths (as in earlier examples), but by arranging the basic colors of one design into a chessboard pattern (Figs. 13, 73). If such alternation is overdone, however, the design becomes too busy. Thus there was a limit to how far this idea could be developed.

*Katami-gawari* and *dan-gawari* were used mainly in Noh costumes, but similar to these were appliqué designs made by sewing on pieces of different cloth and used principally for kosode. The advantage of the appliqué technique was that one could use ready-made materials instead of having to make something especially for the purpose. This made

*119. Noh costume* (atsuita). Dan-gawari *design of cryptomerias with bamboo, chrysanthemum medallions, and checks. Seventeenth or eighteenth century (Edo period). (See also Figure 104.)*

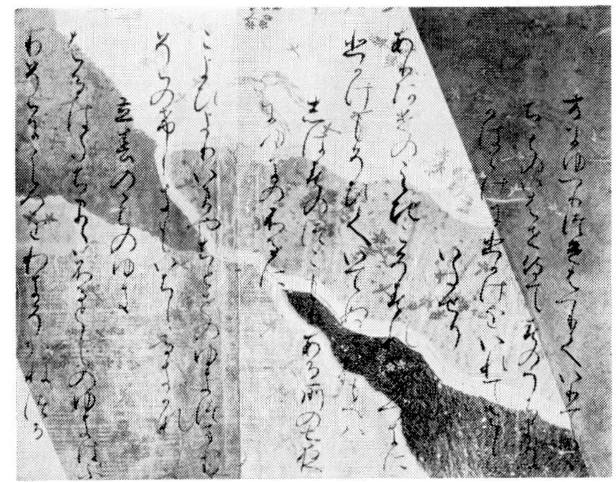

*120. Detail of* Sanjuroku-nin Kashu. *First half of twelfth century. Nishi Hongan-ji, Kyoto.*

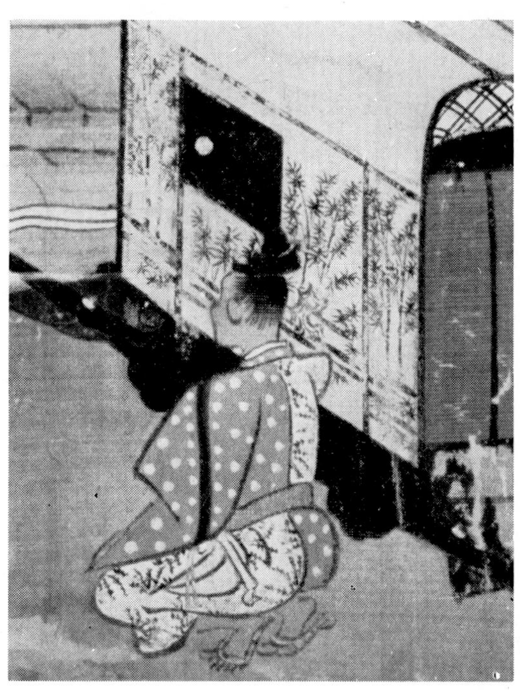

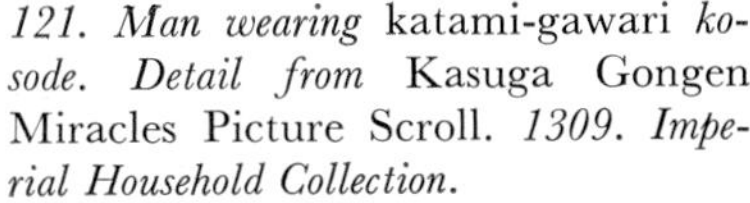

*121. Man wearing* katami-gawari *kosode. Detail from* Kasuga Gongen Miracles Picture Scroll. *1309. Imperial Household Collection.*

for both variety of design and economy. The Temmon kosode (Figs. 35, 123) was not made with this technique but the effect of its tie-dyed and embroidered zigzag design is very similar.

*Kata-suso* (literally, "shoulders and hem") is a type of garment in which a design is placed on the shoulders and at the hem, leaving the rest free of decoration (Fig. 125). *Kata-suso* designs are generally executed in rich embroidery, and since the *kata-suso* type of garment is economical in the sense that no decoration need be applied to the middle section, probably it was a device invented by people of high station when fashionable clothing began to grow inordinately expensive. The undecorated portion of the garment also served to set off the patterned parts at top and bottom, and this would have been another reason for the popularity of this type of garment. The *kata-suso* came to be used not only for Noh costumes but also for ordinary kosode. Because the kosode is invariably worn with an obi, decoration of the middle section is unnecessary, and any embroidery would actually make it difficult to use an obi. However, as fashions became more extravagant, people wanted decoration even where it was superfluous. Nevertheless, because such decoration was meaningless, the pattern was kept simple, emphasis being given to the shoulders or hem and attention turned to variation or contrast between the top and bottom of the garment.

## COMPOSITE, ALLOVER, AND LARGE DESIGNS

Among kosode thought to date from the Muromachi and Momoyama periods, some have designs of rather peculiar composition. These are the so-called *somewake Keicho* kosode (Figs. 34, 101). In these designs we not only have a multitude of circles, rectangles, and triangles superimposed on each other but also all kinds of motifs and techniques existing side by side. There is no standard

*122. Detail of* dofuku *used by Uesugi Kenshin. Patchwork of gold and silver brocades and damask. About 1560 (Muromachi period). Uesugi Shrine, Yamagata Prefecture.*

*123. Detail of kosode (Temmon Kosode) showing embroidered deer and maple sprigs on a black ground. Second half of sixteenth century (Momoyama period). Tokyo National Museum.* ▷

appellation for this type of design, and we do not yet know under what circumstances it developed. I myself use the provisional name "composite designs."

The overall impression gained from these designs is one not of brilliance but of a dense, complex beauty because of the intermingling of various colors and patterns. Because of the preciousness of the cloths used and the great care taken in the way the curves, rectangles, triangles, and other motifs are combined in the composition, we can surmise that these robes were made for women of high rank. They can also be thought of as a type of design created in the transitional period during which the kosode gained its sumptuous character.

The forerunner of this type of design can be seen in the "tear-and-join" paper collages used in the *Sanjuroku-nin Kashu* anthology (Fig. 120) mentioned earlier. Here we see a combination of papers of different colors and designs, sometimes with fuzzy torn edges, sometimes with sharp cut edges. By a natural extension, this design came to be executed with pieces of cloth and with the addition of some new techniques. Thus the composite designs came into being. I mentioned the paper of the *Sanjuroku-nin Kashu* in connection with the *katami-gawari* also, but I do not mean to imply that the idea for these textile designs developed directly from such paper designs. There is a long tradition of this kind of decoration in the history of design. When we recall the loincloths patched together out of old housecloths by Nara-period monks, or how much people treasured the priestly robes called *kesa,* made on the same principle, we see that the Japanese had

an understanding of composite designs and mixed colors from very early times. Indeed, it is characteristic not only of design but also of Japanese culture in general that the composite is preferred to the simple.

In the Muromachi period, a new kind of beauty was created in the mountings of scrolls of calligraphy and paintings by combining imported cloths, such as gold and silver brocades and damask. Thus the ground from which the composite designs were to spring was already prepared. Among the *dofuku* robes used by Uesugi Kenshin is one made up of many different pieces of cloth joined in an irregular fashion (Figs. 36, 122); this is an example of the same kind of design sensibility.

The appearance of this type of design shows that imported cloths were much prized and that large pieces could not be obtained freely. At the same time we can see the desire to use imported stuffs as much as possible in spite of their scarcity. How precious these patchwork garments made from imported materials were can be seen by the fact that Uesugi Kenshin's *dofuku* was a present from Oda Nobunaga; in other words, it was a gift from one warlord at the height of his power to another.

But however much these robes may have been treasured, one gets the feeling that they are overelaborate; they give an impression of triteness (*yabo*). The next development was to be one of refinement and simplification of composite designs. This is represented by the fashion for large designs, which I shall consider next.

The art of the Momoyama period proceeded from an aesthetic of dense composite design to one

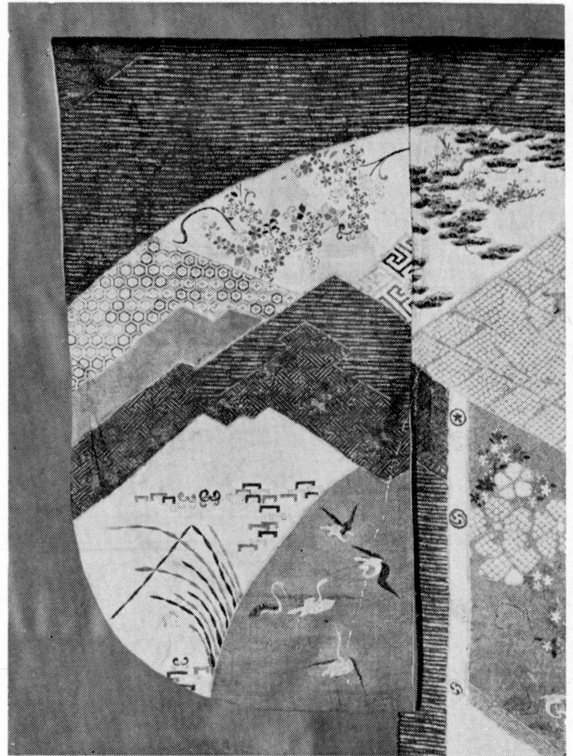

*124. Detail of kosode (one of the* somewake Keicho *kosode). Design of grasses, flowers, and birds of the seasons. About 1600 (Momoyama period). Nagao Art Museum, Tokyo. (See also Figure 9.)*

*125. Noh costume* (nuihaku). Kata-suso *design of paulownias, maple leaves, and mandarin ducks. Second half of sixteenth century (Momoyama period). Kasuga Shrine, Seki, Gifu Prefecture.*

of bold simplicity. It was the genre of partition, screen, and wall paintings that first showed this tendency, and Kano Eitoku (1543–90) was its pioneer. Two works thought to come from his brush are the folding-screen paintings *Kara-shishi* (Chinese Lions) and *Hinoki* (Cypresses). In both Eitoku eliminates extraneous elements, concentrating on beasts and trees. The clarity and boldness seen here are typical of the temper of the Momoyama period. Eitoku's bold, powerful style was to be taken further by the two giants among painters of the time, Hasegawa Tohaku (1539–1610) and Kaiho Yusho (1533–1615), as the style characteristic of the Momoyama period. As one might expect, these developments exerted an influence on textile design, but it took rather a long time for the influence to be felt. In fact, large designs only appeared on the textile scene after the Momoyama period was over.

It may be due to the paucity of garments extant, but the clothes left by people like Toyotomi Hideyoshi, his wife, or Tokugawa Ieyasu—all personalities to whom large, brilliant designs would be suited—do not include any examples of these large designs. The *uchikake* outer robe worn by Hideyoshi's wife (Fig. 126), for instance, has a rich allover design, while Hideyoshi's and Ieyasu's *dofuku*, although simple, give an impression of refinement rather than boldness. Presumably those in positions of greatest power had passed the stage where

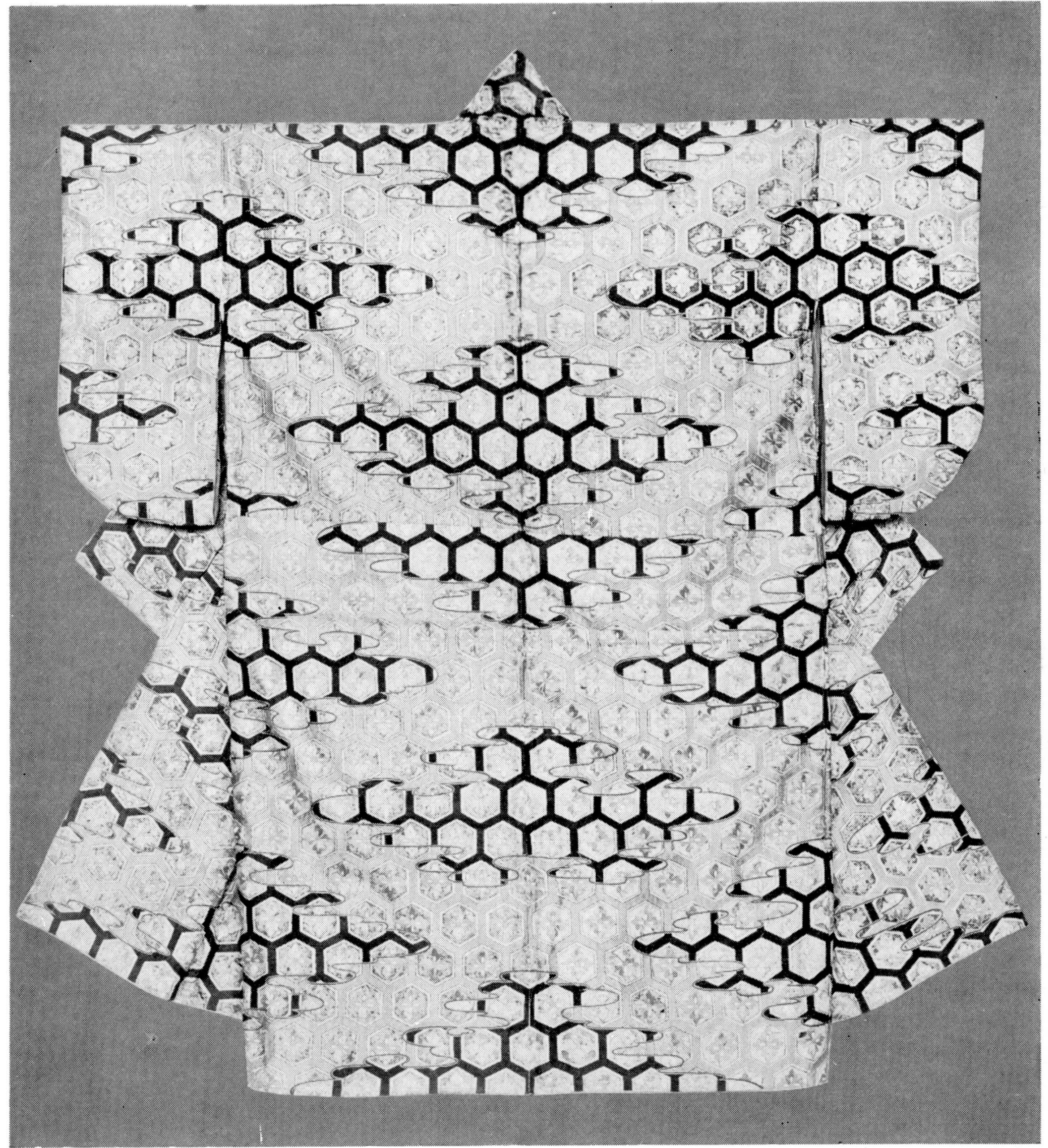

*126.* Uchikake *overrobe used by Toyotomi Hideyoshi's wife. Tortoiseshell-grid design in yellowish green and purple. Second half of sixteenth century (Momoyama period). Kodai-ji, Kyoto.*

they felt a need to express their power through ostentatious dress. Genre paintings of the time, too, show gorgeous costume designs and colors, but no large designs are to be seen.

That the large designs so characteristic of Momoyama taste should only have become popular in the mid-seventeenth century, well after the Momoyama period had ended, may seem paradoxical, but there are reasons for this. When the Momoyama period was over, people felt a nostalgia for its flamboyant mood. There had been a similar feeling of regret at the passing of the age of the Fujiwara clan when that age came to an end in the late twelfth century. In the 1660s large designs were especially popular among the common people, partly because they took pleasure in wearing clothes with such bold designs and partly as a token of resistance to the feudal system, which was becoming ever more inflexible. And the fact that large designs involved less work than composite ones was another factor that increased their popularity among the masses.

A large design that is merely an enlargement of part of an allover design is not very effective. The special character of the large designs of the Edo period comes from the fact that a single motif or small group of motifs is extracted from an allover design and is depicted clearly on a larger scale. The undecorated areas left by this method serve as a foil to the motif. The proportion of plain ground to decoration is different on the front and back of the garment, but at least two-thirds of the total area is left undecorated. If the plain area were reduced, the special character of the large

*127. Detail of kosode. Purple figured silk; design of waves and carp. Seventeenth or eighteenth century (Edo period).*

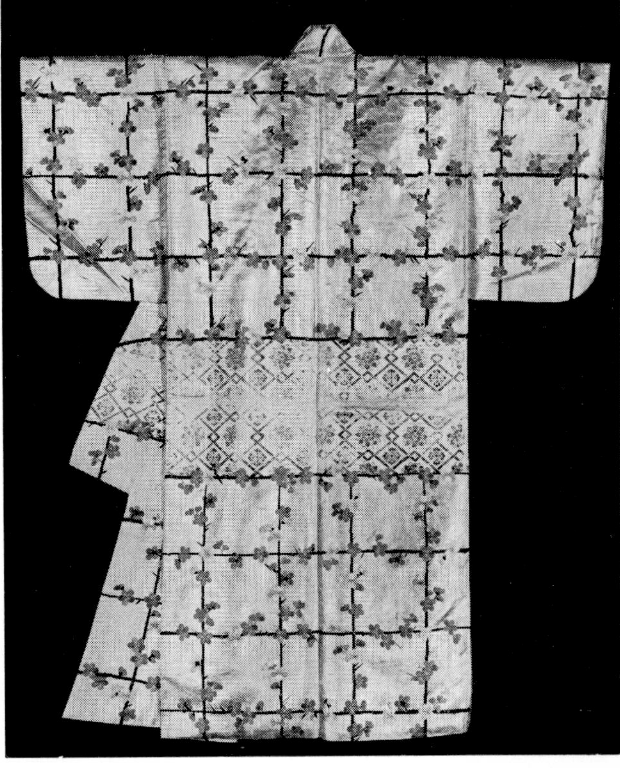

*128. Noh costume* (nuihaku). Koshi-gawari *design of trellis with red cherry blossoms on gold ground. Seventeenth or eighteenth century (Edo period).*

motif would be vitiated, and the whole design would take on a *yabo* flavor. The division between the ground and the design usually takes the form of an arc dividing the area into one-quarter of design and three-quarters of plain ground. The design is so placed that one sleeve has a design while the other sleeve is left plain, and part of the hem has a diagonal design while the rest is plain. It can be considered a diagonal variant of the *katami-gawari* principle. This version of the *katami-gawari* now became one of the basic forms of kosode design.

Originally, the novelty of the large designs lay in the simple treatment of the motifs, and this was also the reason for their popularity. However, the aristocracy and wealthy merchants were not satisfied with this, and eventually *kanoko* allover tie-dyed versions of large motifs were produced. The kosode shown in Figure 76, once owned by Tokugawa Iemitsu's concubine Keisho-in, is a good example. Although we know from paintings that many of the large designs were very simple in treatment, the majority of garments extant are of the more luxurious variety.

SCATTERED MOTIFS *Chirashi-moyo,* or "scattered-motif designs," are another important category of textile decoration. Although designs of this type are rather different from the large-motif designs, the two have something in common—both can be described as resulting from a process of enlarging one part of an allover design, and in both a considerable area of undecorated background plays an important part

*129. Kosode. White figured satin; design of flowing water, chrysanthemums, and wisterias. About 1700 (Edo period). Tokyo National Museum. (See also Figure 39.)*

*130 (opposite page, left). Hon'ami Koetsu. Writing box with* maki-e *design of pontoon bridge. Seventeenth century (early Edo period). Tokyo National Museum.* ▷

*131 (opposite page, right). Noh costume* (atsuita). Katami-gawari *design of characters from poems in gold-on-red and red-on-gold. Momoyama Period. Tokyo National Museum.* ▷

in the overall effect. Scattered-motif designs were an important form of costume decoration in Edo-period Japan, but they were already known as far back as the Nara and Heian periods, as well as in the ancient West.

Still, Japanese scattered designs have unique features in the motifs used and in the manner of composition. Orderly arrangement of the units of a design existed both in the East and in the West in ancient times. This type appeared in Japan too but was never popular. Instead, what might be called a distortion of such arrangements, consisting of a free distribution of groups of motifs, was considered more elegant. The same kind of sensibility is to be seen in the form of calligraphy called *chirashi-gaki* ("scattered writing"), popular in the Nara and Heian periods. In this, the vertical columns do not necessarily start or finish at the same height, nor are they always perfectly vertical or straight. The same device of irregularity is found in applied arts other than costume, too. The papers used for the writing of poetic anthologies and sutras were decorated with scattered motifs of flowers and grasses, as were the insides of the lids of lacquer boxes for stationery and other small items.

But if motifs are merely arranged at random the result is neither beautiful nor artistic. The motifs must be of the right size and number, and their arrangement, though not regular, should be balanced. In addition, and this may be something that only the Japanese understand, the motifs chosen must have a poetic suggestiveness about them. Scattered blossoms and birds, for example,

may have universal appeal, but they are too commonplace and trite, too lacking in poetic qualities to be suitable motifs for this type of design.

A superb example of a scattered-motif design can be seen in the *atsuita* Noh costume shown in Figure 131. This is a *katami-gawari* robe of pure and bold conception, half consisting of a red ground with a design of scattered characters woven in gold thread, the other half having red characters woven on a gold ground. Skillfully balanced with regard to placement, size, and thickness of strokes, the characters are lines from the *Wakan Roei Shu,* an eleventh-century Japanese anthology of Japanese and Chinese poetry. Scattered-character designs had already been seen in the *ashide-e* designs of the Heian period. Typically, these took the form of characters scattered throughout waterside scenes in such a way that the strokes of the characters were incorporated into the outlines of rocks, trees, reeds, and so on. *Ashide-e* designs were often used on decorated writing papers. The scattered-motif device was also used in Kamakura-period *maki-e* (lacquerware with designs in gold and silver dust). The painter, calligrapher, and potter Hon'ami Koetsu (1558–1637) was particularly skilled at scattered-character designs, and the *maki-e* writing box shown in Figure 130 is an example of his work in this style.

Another, rather different, type of scattered-character design is shown in the kosode of Figure 132. Not as pure a form of the scattered-motif genre as the Noh costume of Figure 131, this and similar types of design appear to have been much liked by the Edo-period Japanese. The design consists of

*132. Kosode. White figured satin; Kaga* yuzen *design of maple sprigs and the character for "deer." Seventeenth or eighteenth century (mid-Edo period).*

scattered maple leaves in autumn colors with the character for "deer" distributed among them. In the Temmon kosode (Fig. 123) the same motifs can be seen, but in this case both leaves and deer are represented pictorically. In the kosode of Figure 132, however, the deer are represented indirectly, in the form of characters. This indirect, allusive representation by means of characters would seem to have something in common with *iki* taste. The Kaigetsudo school of ukiyo-e artists were fond of depicting courtesans wearing kosode with scattered-character designs.

The next most common type of scattered-motif design is *semmen-chirashi,* or "scattered fans." As far back as the Heian period, the folding fan had been an accessory popular with high and low alike, and its appearance as a design motif also goes back a long time. In scattered-fan designs (Fig. 139) the fans are shown fully open, closed, and at various intermediate stages. The overall effect is reminiscent of the elegant diversion of fan floating, in which beautifully decorated fans would be floated down a stream for the appreciation of those gathered for the occasion.

Another popular type of design is *shikishi-chirashi* (scattered *shikishi*). This too is reminiscent of elegant courtly pastimes. *Shikishi* are roughly square pieces of paper or cards for painting or writing poetry on. In the Heian period they were pasted on folding-screen paintings, and on them were written poems relevant and complementary to the subjects of the paintings. Eventually, instead of

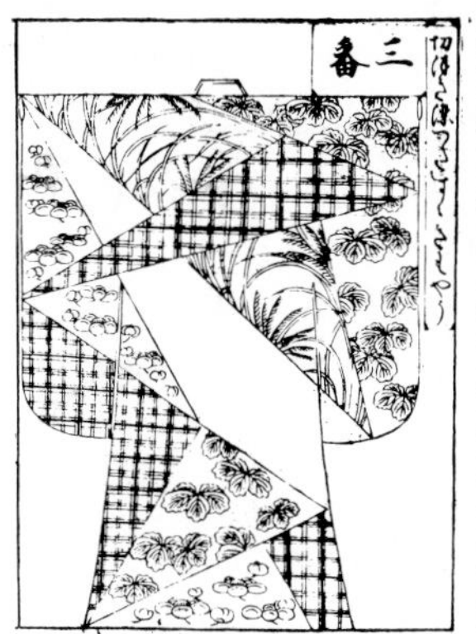


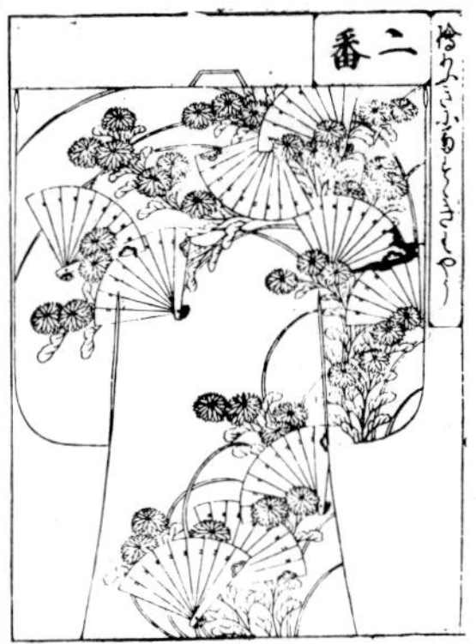


*133. Two pages from kosode design book* (Tanzen Hiina-gata Taisei). *1704.*

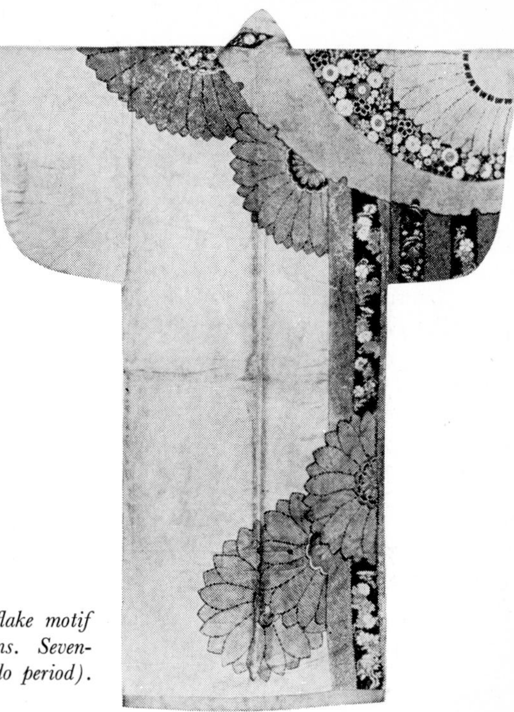

*134. Kosode. Design of snowflake motif* (yukiwa) *and chrysanthemums. Seventeenth century (first half of Edo period). Nagao Art Museum, Tokyo.*

pasting real *shikishi* on to paintings, square areas of the painting surface were left unpainted, and poems were written in these. The harmonious "scattering" of these *shikishi* added to the interest of the paintings, and so it is not surprising that the tradition was adopted in the field of textile design. The use of scattered *shikishi* in the grapevine design of the *surihaku* Noh costume of Figure 97 gives the design a poetic richness. In the Edo period, with the addition of *tanzaku* (narrow rectangular cards or shapes representing these; Fig. 110), this type of scattered design gained greater variety.

Japanese family crests, which are commonly circular medallions, were popular in scattered-motif designs in the Edo period. Circular motifs have a long history in Japanese textile design, dating back to the Heian period in the form of such designs as phoenix, butterfly, and crane medallions. But scattered designs of family crests were typical decorative devices of the Edo period. These crests originated in ordinary scattered-motif designs, some of whose motifs gradually came to be associated with particular families. As feudal society developed, increasing importance was attached to the family crest, and corresponding to this tendency, crests appeared as decorative motifs on textiles.

These designs used not real family crests but medallion motifs suggestive of crests. This allowed greater liberty for variations and color permutations. Especially when used on a black ground, scattered-crest designs had a dramatic beauty. These designs are now firmly established, and in Noh and dance costumes (Fig. 135), they still cap-

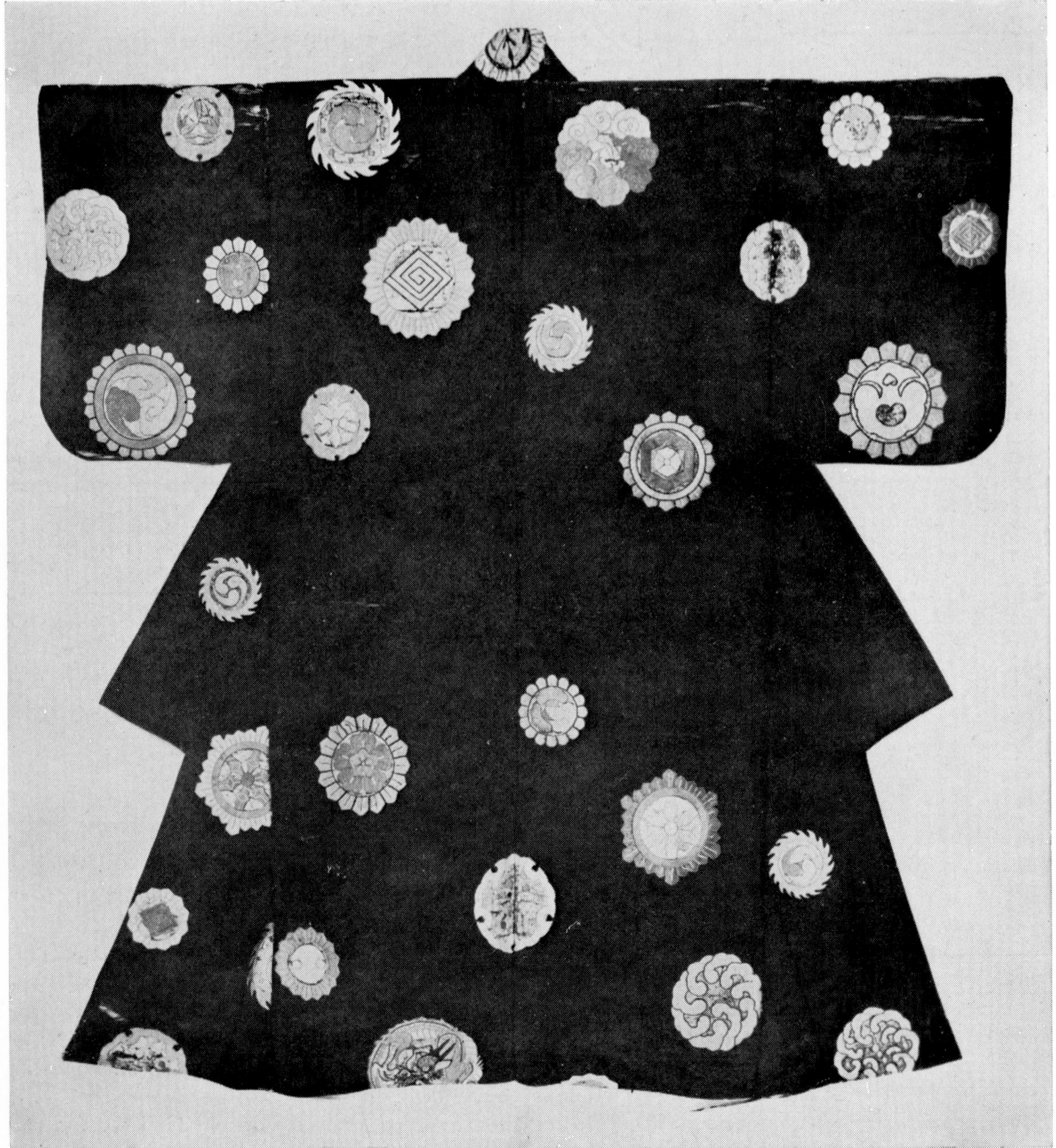

*135. Noh costume* (nuihaku). *Design of scattered crest medallions on black ground. Seventeenth or eighteenth century (Edo period). Tokugawa Art Museum, Nagoya.*

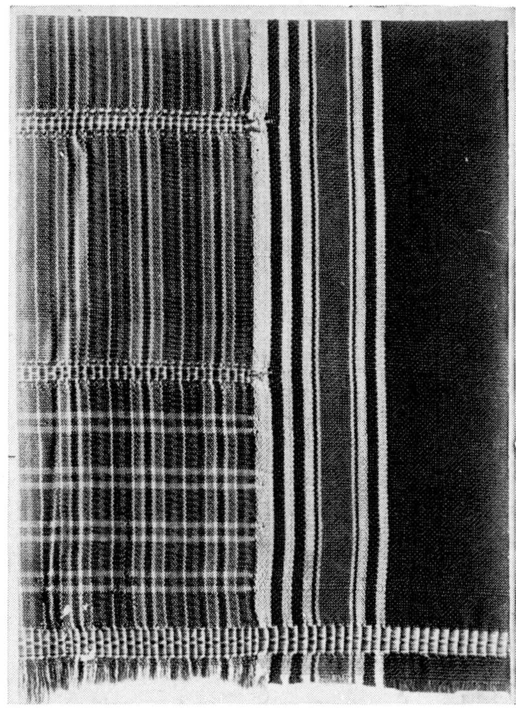

*136. Fragment of* kanto *striped fabric known as Mochizuki Kanto.*

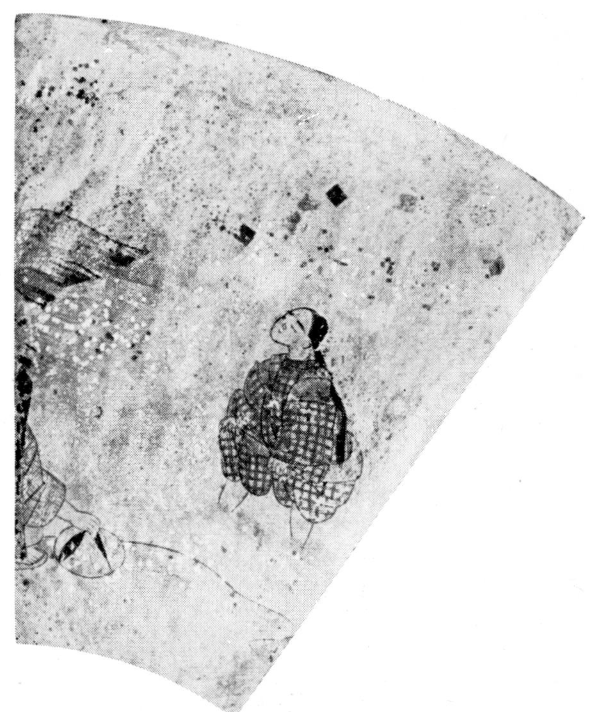

*137. Detail of sutra fan. Second half of twelfth century. Shitenno-ji, Osaka.*

tivate audiences. It is recorded that around the 1660s, a famous geisha named Usuyuki wore a robe with a design of medallions on a red ground of figured satin. In the medallions were embroidered the forty-eight signs of the Japanese syllabic script. This represented a skillful combination of the scattered-character and scattered-crest types of design.

In the course of time, scattered-crest designs that broke with previous conventions were invented. Medallions of grasses and flowers, in particular, appeared in endless variety. Accompanying the development of pictorial designs, to be described later, there appeared designs consisting of parts of a landscape scattered over a garment. When the pictorial representation remains stylized and simple, these are effective, but when the treatment is more realistic, their impact as design is lost.

STRIPES AND CHECKS In spite of the simplicity of striped and checked designs, very few old examples remain, and there are very few pictorial representations of people wearing clothes made from such material. The fan-sutra painting illustrated in Figure 137, showing a servant dressed in a garment with a check design, is one of the few extant examples. The reason for this seems to have been that because these designs were easy to weave and were readily available even to people of lowly status, they were looked down on. Thus the aristocracy of ancient Japan never knew the beauty of simple stripes and checks.

*138. Detail of Noh costume* (nuihaku). *Design of paulownia leaves and phoenix medallions on red ground. Eighteenth century (mid-Edo period). Tokugawa Art Museum, Nagoya.*

Although stripes and checks require only the simplest of weaving techniques, it is precisely their simplicity and clarity that give them their beauty. The Japanese were first attracted by this beauty in the Muromachi period, when striped and checked fabrics were imported from Ming China and Europe. These high-quality striped fabrics were called *kanto* (Fig. 136). The famous tea master Kobori Enshu (1579–1647) was particularly fond of them and boldly introduced these exotic fabrics into the tea ceremony. They were used for bags in which *cha-ire* (small ceramic caddies for powdered tea) and tea bowls were kept when not in use. The high proportion of *kanto* fabrics among extant tea-utensil bags suggests how highly they were thought of. Because of the popularity of these fabrics, high-quality striped and checked weaves began to be produced in Japan also, and the generals of the Momoyama period wore clothing made from these materials. At the same time, considerable quantities of less expensive versions of these stuffs were made for the common people, and clothes with these designs appear frequently in genre paintings of the Muromachi and early Edo periods. In 1787 the shogunate gave special permission for subjects of samurai status to wear striped fabrics, which suggests that most kinds of striped fabrics were still considered beneath the dignity of a samurai.

Striped and checked designs are most effective when they use bold, vivid color combinations. In the paintings of the Muromachi and early Edo periods, even men are sometimes shown wearing

*139. Detail of Noh costume* (karaori). *Design of* karakusa *scrolls and scattered fans on red ground. Seventeenth or eighteenth century (Edo period). Shinshiro Noh Society, Aichi Prefecture.*

clothing with designs that include red stripes, in spite of the fact that red was traditionally considered a "feminine" color. A great variety of striped designs can be obtained by using different numbers and combinations of colors and by varying the width of the stripes. This produces an abstract rather than a representational beauty, and it is strange that the Japanese did not awake earlier to this type of effect, for it was certainly within their technical capabilities. Even today, however, when abstract art is in vogue, the striking effect of stripes and checks is not acknowledged as much as might be expected.

Fortunately, the beauty of stripes and checks was immediately recognized and preserved in Noh costume. This is partly because Noh and Kyogen costumes represented and transmitted fairly accurately the actual dress styles of the Muromachi and Momoyama periods. But part of the reason must have been that the abstract nature of stripes and checks blended well with the "phantasmic" character of Noh performances. In addition to utilizing existing designs, Noh was responsible for the creation of a number of fine new stripe and check designs (Figs. 102, 104, 128, 140, 142). Their bold and brilliant color schemes give an astonishingly modern impression, and they represent one of the great contributions of Noh costume to Japanese textile design.

Once such high-quality cloths were being produced, woven motifs began to be incorporated into the area between the stripes. Although this made

*140. Detail of Noh costume* (surihaku). *Tortoiseshell-grid design on striped ground. Seventeenth or eighteenth century (Edo period).*

*141. Detail from landscape painting on hemp cloth. Eighth century. Shoso-in, Nara.*

*142. Detail of Noh costume* (atsuita). Dan-gawari *design of checks and chrysanthemums, and stripes. Seventeenth or eighteenth century (Edo period). Tokugawa Art Museum, Nagoya.*

for greater variety, it also had the unfortunate effect of spoiling the purity of these designs.

PICTORIAL DESIGNS Pictorial designs, as opposed to geometric or other stylized designs, are a characteristic feature of Japanese textiles as well as other applied arts. Many Noh costumes and kosode have pictorial decorations. Although designs with one or more pictorial motifs repeated all over the garment exist, most typically one large motif, such as a flowering tree or one landscape scene, spreads over the whole garment.

These kinds of pictorial designs were popular with the Japanese, but they were not necessarily invented by the Japanese. In T'ang-period China, for example, hunt motifs were popular. They were applied as decoration to all kinds of vessels and other articles and exerted an influence on Japanese designs of the Nara period. Trays decorated in litharge pigments and landscapes painted on hemp cloth (Fig. 141) dating from the Nara period have been preserved in the Shoso-in repository at Nara and illustrate well the characteristics of pictorical designs of those times.

The popularity of pictorial designs in the Heian period was due to the fact that the aesthetic ideal of the court at that time was the quality called *aware,* a sense of melancholy and pathos in connection with beauty, and this ideal was naturally pursued in the decorative arts as well. The artists of the so-called Japanese style of painting (*yama-*

*143. Chest with* maki-e *design of plovers in a marsh. Twelfth century. Kongobu-ji, Wakayama Prefecture.*

*to-e*) were skilled at expressing *aware,* and their paintings were suited for use as decoration on boxes and other vessels. The small chest with a *maki-e* lacquer design of plovers in a marsh (Fig. 143) is a good example of this. Japanese bronze mirrors of the period also often used pictorial designs for decoration.

In the Kamakura period the ability to create effective stylized designs decreased somewhat, and pictorial designs became the main type of decoration. But since in this period the political and social center of gravity shifted from the court aristocracy to the samurai warrior class, it is not surprising that the courtly effect called *aware* diminished. Pictorial designs remained popular in the Muromachi period and later, but they were based on a different conception. In the Muromachi and Momoyama periods painting itself became decorative in character, thus lessening the difference between pictorial and stylized designs. For example, among paintings of these two periods there are many, like the pair of screens *Landscape with Sun and Moon* at the Kongo-ji temple (Osaka) and the pair of screens called *The Bridge at Uji* (Fig. 146), that could be used as kimono designs with no adaptation. The pictorial designs of these periods were simplified or even distorted for decorative purposes and as such had a special appeal and interest of their own.

In the Edo period pictorial designs became even more popular. One factor that helped this form of decoration to become popular was that easily comprehensible pictures were felt to be more familiar than stylized designs. In addition, it was easier for a designer to create a pictorial representation than a stylized one. The invention of the paste-resist method of dyeing known as *yuzen-zome* must have been another important factor, for by this technique it was possible to recreate in textiles something of the feeling of the brushwork and colors of actual painting. Once subtle effects like shading became possible in dyeing, pictorial designs were drowned in a sea of technique. When technical progress is not accompanied by stylization, we

*144.* Katabira. *Flowing water and plants on indigo ground. Seventeenth or eighteenth century (Edo period). Suntory Art Museum, Tokyo.*

*145.* Katabira. Chaya-zome *dyed design of the type called* gosho-toki. *Seventeenth or eighteenth century (Edo period).*

*146. Detail from* The Bridge at Uji. *Pair of folding screens. Second half of sixteenth century (Momoyama period). Tokyo National Museum.*

tend to find the simplified and stylized types of design developed earlier, when technical limitations did not allow so much freedom, more interesting. Overelaboration is one of the unfortunate effects of technical progress and was the cause of the decline of not only design but also Kyoto painting as such. It required many years and a considerable effort before the painters of Kyoto were able to free themselves from the *yuzen-zome* style of painting.

In the process of the general vulgarization of pictorial designs, the type known as *chaya-zome* is noteworthy as an exception. With its simple color scheme, predominantly indigo on white, it was popular because of its eminent suitability for summer wear. One other point worthy of attention in the bold and simple pictorial designs of *chaya-zome* is that many depict rustic landscapes. Skillful treatment of the shapes of complex buildings is often apparent, so that together with the simplicity of technique there is a rich poetic suggestiveness. *Chaya-zome* was a unique style, different from that of the Kano school, at that time a powerful influence in painting circles, and from those of the Rimpa (Korin), Maruyama, and Shijo schools of painting. Probably it was developed by the *chaya-zome* dyers themselves in their struggles with the limitations of the techniques available to them. We see here a close connection between pictorial designs and textile techniques and can but admire the genius of the anonymous designers of *chaya-zome*.

CHAPTER SIX

# Techniques and Motifs of Japanese Textiles

We must not forget that behind the beauty of the kosode and Noh costume lies Japan's outstanding tradition of weaving and dyeing techniques. Kosode and Noh costumes are both beautiful to look at from a distance and pleasant to touch. This is not only due to the feel of the silks from which they are made; it comes also from the technical refinement resulting from their creators' long experience. A new technique may seem to have been invented suddenly, but on investigation we usually find that it has a long tradition behind it. When a fine tradition seems to have died out, it emerges again like a phoenix from the ashes. Traditional techniques appear again and again in new guises in response to the demands of the fashions of a new age. In the following section, I would like to outline major aspects of the technical tradition in order to give the reader a deeper insight into the evolution of the kosode and Noh costume.

## SURIHAKU AND NUIHAKU

*Surihaku,* literally "printed foil" or "impressed foil," refers to designs executed by applying sheets of gold or silver leaf to cloth or other materials. Sometimes this technique is simply called *haku* (foil). It was a popular method of costume decoration from the Muromachi to the early Edo period. The material was usually satin of the *shusu* or *rinzu* type. A stencil of the desired design is placed on the cloth and paste is applied through this, after which the stencil is removed. Gold or silver leaf is placed over the paste while it is still wet. When the paste has dried, any superfluous foil is removed. In order to show the silver or gold of the design to best advantage, the cloth used is usually deep red, purple, or indigo. On most of the examples we have today, much of the foil has rubbed away, leaving only a dull sheen, but even this enables us to imagine how beautifully it must have shone when new. It seems quite natural that the type of Noh costume decorated by this technique and itself called *surihaku* should be used mainly for female roles.

The origins of the *surihaku* technique can be traced to Nara times. Some tapestries of this period have gold-leaf decoration. *Eiga Monogatari* (A Tale of Glory) describes robes decorated by the *surihaku* method as part of the sumptous court attire. But there were special reasons for this technique's sudden rise in popularity in the Muromachi period. During the Kamakura and Muromachi periods, gold and silver brocade (*kinran* and *ginran*), as well as a type of loose gauze with designs woven in gold or silver thread (known as *takeyamachi,* after the section of Kyoto in which it subsequently came to be made) were very popular. These materials

*147. Detail of Noh costume* (nuihaku). *Design of reeds and boats on indigo ground. Seventeenth or eighteenth century (Edo period). Shinshiro Noh Society, Aichi Prefecture.*

were imported from China and were scarce and highly valued. Zen monks, who at the time enjoyed a high social status, used them for their robes. Eventually, in the Momoyama period, such cloths were also produced in Japan, but before the skill of Japanese weavers had reached that level it was necessary to find a substitute technique. That technique was *surihaku.*

As I mentioned earlier, *surihaku* had predecessors as far back as the Nara period, but it is doubtful whether people of the Muromachi period knew of these. A factor that must have influenced the emergence of *surihaku* was a fabric called *inkin* ("stamped gold"), which was being imported from China in the Muromachi period. *Inkin* was valued for use in the mountings of calligraphy and paintings, and many examples have been preserved in that form. *Inkin* designs in gold or silver leaf are applied to silk material of loose weave by a method similar to that of *surihaku,* but what distinguishes the two is that *surihaku* designs are generally larger than those of *inkin.* Another difference is that whereas *inkin* was applied to a special loose-weave fabric, *surihaku* was used on the *shusu* and *rinzu* satins in common use during Muromachi times. Compared with *kinran* and *ginran* brocades, whose woven designs were built up out of narrow gold and silver threads, the method of *surihaku* decora-

*148 (top). Fragment of Buddhist monk's stole. Imported from China;* inkin *gold-leaf design of peony scrolls and Buddhist emblems. Mid-fifteenth century (Ming dynasty). Nanzen-ji, Kyoto.*

*149 (center). Detail of* kinran *gold brocade imported from China. Woven design of gold flowers on red ground. Thirteenth century (Southern Sung dynasty). Tokyo National Museum.*

*150 (bottom). Detail of gift wrapper* (fukusa). *Embroidered auspicious design on red damask ground. Second half of seventeenth century (early Edo period). Kombu-in, Nara.*

tion was very simple. The popularity of *surihaku* was no doubt due to its visual effect, but the fact that this type of cloth was easily obtainable was a contributing influence. What with the general Momoyama predilection for brilliant gold coloring and the sudden increase in gold production at that time, the popularity of *surihaku* is easily understood.

The *surihaku* Noh costume with a design of grapevines and *shikishi* of Figure 97 exhibits the beauty of *surihaku* in a pure form; the choice of a deep purple cloth was intended to bring to life the gold of the decoration. The use of stencils to apply the paste to the fabric makes for fast and therefore economical production, but of course this means that the same motif or pattern is used repeatedly. In the case of the grapevine *surihaku,* however, stencils were cut especially for this garment. Thus although *surihaku* is usually associated with relatively inexpensive garments, there are some, like this one, of very high quality.

*151. Noh costume* (surihaku). *Gold-leaf scale design on a red ground. Seventeenth or eighteenth century (Edo period). Tokugawa Art Museum, Nagoya.*

*152. Scene from a performance of the Noh play* Aoi no Ue.

Another distinctive type of *surihaku* decoration is the triangular *uroko* design. The scalelike triangle motifs of this pattern are suggestive of the scales (*uroko*) of a serpent, and costumes with this design are typically used for female-demon roles in Noh. Figure 151 shows a *surihaku* of this type used for the *shite* (protagonist) role in the play *Dojo-ji*. The design is in gold on a red ground, aptly symbolic of the vengeful passion of a serpent-woman. Figure 152 shows a scene from *Aoi no Ue* (Lady Aoi), in which the jealous spirit of Lady Rokujo beats Lady Aoi, her young rival for the love of Prince Genji, with her fan. (Note that Lady Aoi is supposed to be on her sickbed and is represented by a folded kosode laid out on the floor of the stage.) In Noh, the *surihaku* represents an undergarment, and here it is hidden for the most part by the *karaori* worn over it but can be seen at the chest. In this case the design is in silver leaf on a white ground—a combination of colors that one would normally not expect to work well. But because it helps to create a cold, ghostly atmosphere, it is highly suited to the role of Lady Rokujo.

One garment that particularly shows the novelty and originality of *surihaku* is the *noshime* Noh costume of Figure 68. Here the *surihaku* decoration itself, applied over a basic design of horizontal stripes, is simple, but the foil against the multicolored background creates a crisp effect.

*Nuihaku* is a combination of *surihaku* and embroidery. Superficially *surihaku* seems to have the same kind of effect as gold and silver brocades, but on close comparison we find there is a difference. Inasmuch as the motifs in brocades are made up of gold and silver threads woven into the fabric of the material, their brightness has a certain sense of mass or weight. *Surihaku,* on the other hand, inevitably gives an impression of flatness. In the first stages of the development of *nuihaku* from *surihaku,* touches of embroidery were added here and

*153. Detail of imported* kinran *gold brocade. Design of peony scroll in gold on indigo ground. About 1370 (Ming dynasty). Tokyo National Museum.*

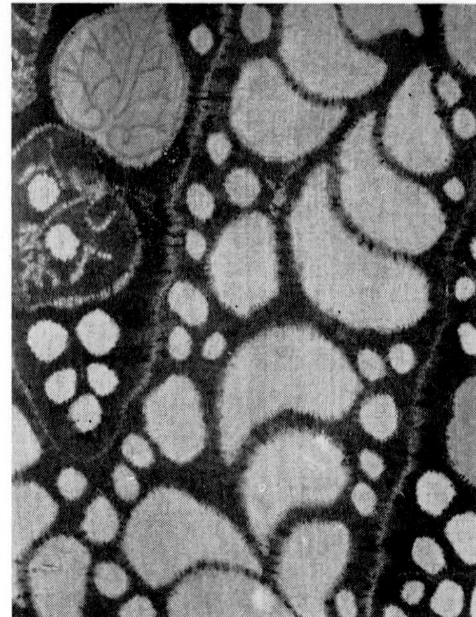

*154. Detail of kosode material. Pongee* (tsumugi); tsujigahana *dyed design of wisterias and hollyhocks. Sixteenth century (Muromachi or Momoyama period).*

there to alleviate the flatness. Eventually the proportion of embroidery increased, until the *surihaku* decoration had only a secondary importance. Finally, the gold and silver took the form of threads used in the embroidery rather than appliquéd foil, and so *surihaku* made its exit from the world of costume. The rather unusual figured-satin kosode shown in Figure 109 is considered a *nuihaku*. The *surihaku* method of decoration is attractive not only when it carries the principal design but even when it consists of only a small section of the overall pattern.

## TSUJIGAHANA AND TIE-DYEING

In the Muromachi and Momoyama periods, when *surihaku* was at the height of its glory, it played a part in the development of a type of decoration known as *tsujigahana*. These designs, consisting of a combination of tie-dyed, hand-painted, and *surihaku* elements, are a distinctive form of textile decoration that flourished in the Muromachi and Momoyama periods. Tie-dyeing is without a doubt the most important technique involved; so in order to understand the rise of *tsujigahana* fabrics we must first know something of tie-dyeing techniques.

*Shibori-zome* (tie-dyeing) is a very old method of decorating textiles, and tie-dyed fabrics have been found among the textile fragments left by ancient peoples. In Nara-period Japan a wide range of tie-dyeing techniques from primitive to sophisticated were known. They are known by the term *kokechi*, and many examples of fabrics dyed by these methods are preserved in the Shoso-in repository. Although we have no extant examples from the Heian or Kamakura period, we know from picture scrolls depicting the customs and manners of those periods that tie-dyeing was practiced. One of the applications of tie-dyed fabrics shown in these scrolls is the edge bindings of folding screens. In

*155. Detail of kosode material. Blue figured satin; tie-dyed design of crane medallions in* kanoko *spots. First half of nineteenth century (late Edo period).*

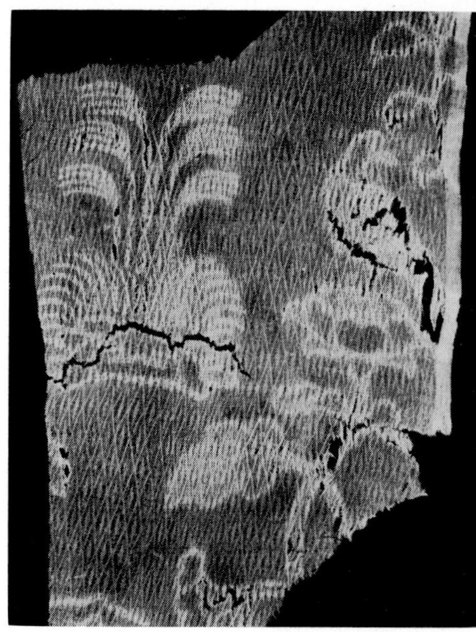

*156. Fragment of gauze decorated with the* kyokechi *block-resist dyeing method. Design of flowers and birds. Eighth century. Tokyo National Museum.*

the Nara period, brocades had been commonly used for this purpose, but in the Heian period the technically simpler tie-dyed fabrics also came into use. No doubt this was considered novel and somewhat unconventional at the time and was welcomed for this reason. In her *Makura no Soshi* (Pillow Book), the eleventh-century court lady Sei Shonagon gives a list including the following kinds of dyed fabrics: *maki-zome, murago,* and *kukuri-zome*—all types of tie-dyeing. *Maki-zome* (literally, "wound dyeing") was a simple technique executed by winding cords around a roll of cloth, after which the roll was dyed. The parts compressed by the cords remained their natural color. In *murago,* different shades of the same color merge into each other. *Kukuri-zome* refers to finely executed tie-dyed designs. In the *Eiga Monogatari* (A Tale of Glory), mentioned earlier, there are references to textiles that may be tie-dyed.

The decorated paper used for the so-called fan sutras, thought to have been made from the end of the Heian period into the Kamakura period, show men and women of low social status wearing costumes decorated with *kanoko* tie-dyed designs and the tie-dyed indigo designs called *mitsume* and *yotsume.* Similar designs are depicted in such works as the picture scrolls *Ippen Shonin Eden* (Pictorial Biography of Saint Ippen) and *Honen Shonin Eden* (Pictorial Biography of Saint Honen). Whereas the tie-dyed fabrics used for trimming folding screens in palaces and mansions were of many colors, with the passage of time the technique became more popular and the designs were reduced to simple ones in indigo alone.

Tie-dyeing became truly popular in the Muromachi period. There are thought to have been two main reasons for this. One was the appearance of the kosode type of garment, for this provided a good medium for tie-dyed designs. The other was technical progress in tie-dyeing methods. More

*157. Detail of kosode material. Light-blue glossed silk;* tsujigahana *dyed design of grasses and flowers in areas defined by "pine bark" zigzag lines. Second half of sixteenth century (Momoyama period).*

specifically, multicolor designs became possible, and the *nuishime-shibori* technique was developed. In this, the bunches of cloth were sewn up to prevent the dye from seeping in, instead of being tied up. This gave the dyer considerable freedom in the colors and shapes he could use in his designs. However, because this technique was still basically a form of tie-dyeing, the outlines of the design were fuzzy. Moreover, the parts of the material left undyed gave a feeling of something empty that needed to be filled. It was at this point that the idea of adding hand-painted designs was conceived.

Why this composite of tie-dyed and hand-painted designs should be called *tsujigahana* is not clear. The meaning is something like "flowers at the crossing," and it is possible that the earliest designs of this type consisted of some kind of tie-dyed lattice pattern at the intersections (*tsuji*) of which hand-painted flowers or similar motifs were added. If this was the case, then "flowers at the crossing" is a very apposite name. Many *tsujigahana* designs include a lozenge motif with a zigzag outline called *matsukawa-bishi* ("pine-bark diamond"; Figs. 96, 157, and Foldout 2) in thick *sumi* (Chinese ink). This seems to represent a vestige or modification of a lattice or trellis pattern intersecting on the diagonal. Very few examples of such a diagonal-lattice prototype are to be seen, but most of even the earliest examples extant represent a fairly advanced stage of *tsujigahana*. It is thus unfortunately impossible to say what early *tsujigahana* textiles were like.

Turning our attention to the aesthetic aspect of *tsujigahana,* what does its beauty consist in? Why did the Japanese of the Muromachi and Momoyama periods find it so appealing? The answers to these questions lie in the refreshing effect of the contrast and at the same time the harmony of the tie-dyed and hand-painted elements, and in the relationship of the soft, hazy shapes of tie-dyeing to the fine, sharply etched line of the hand-painted motifs. Sometimes color is used for the hand-painted motifs, but usually a fine black-ink line is used. The motifs are generally flowers and birds. There is a touch of sadness about the bright quality

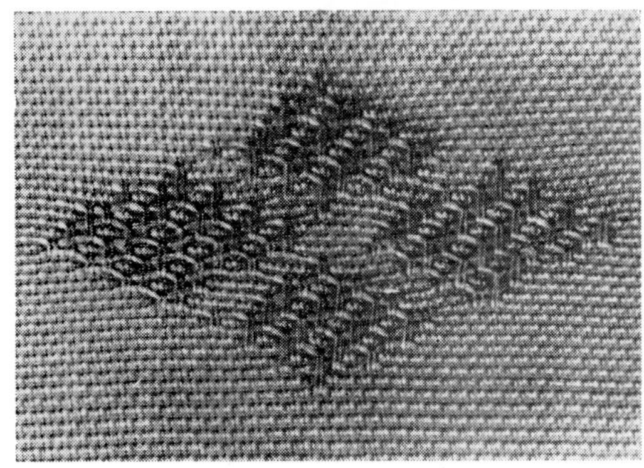

*158. Detail of quadruple-lozenge* yusoku *pattern. Gauze.*

*159. Detail of Noh costume* (nuihaku). *Design of grapes and* karahana *("Chinese flower") motifs. Second half of sixteenth century (Momoyama period). Tokyo National Museum.*

*160. Detail of Noh costume* (atsuita). *Design of nested squares and* umban *motifs on zigzag* yamagata *("mountain forms") ground. Seventeenth century (early Edo period). Tokugawa Art Museum, Nagoya.*

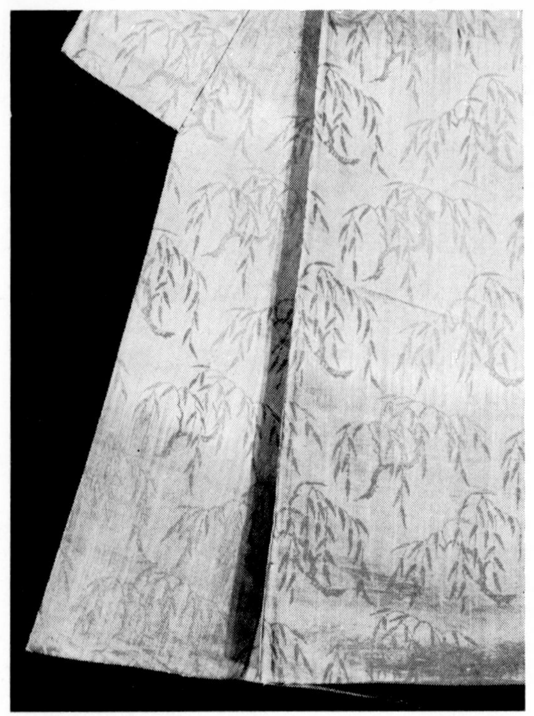

of *tsujigahana* that strikes us as elegant and graceful. This resembles the Noh, which sought the "flower" (beauty) in the mysterious, graceful quality called *yugen*.

Once *tsujigahana* had gained recognition, the formerly humble technique was gradually refined into something sophisticated. The tie-dyed element became more complicated, and hand-painted motifs, originally linear designs, began to incorporate delicate shading. This can be seen quite clearly in the petal outlines of the designs shown in Figures 79, 96, and 157. Another development was the use of vermilion and green for the designs, whereas previously only black ink had been used. This made for more colorful designs but at the same time weakened the contrastive and complementary effect of the two distinct elements of *tsujigahana*. Eventually *surihaku* and embroidery were also added. With these developments the pure beauty of the original *tsujigahana* was lost. Ultimately, even the diagonal lattices and the zigzag "pine bark" lozenges—those vestiges of the origins of the very name *tsujigahana*—disappear.

The fact that among the extant *dofuku* of people like Uesugi Kenshin, Toyotomi Hideyoshi, and Tokugawa Ieyasu are some with a *tsujigahana* design (Figs. 26, 33, 78) indicates how universally loved and refined these designs had become by their time. But this was a sad result of their rise to fame. In Hideyoshi's and Ieyasu's *dofuku* robes only vestiges of hand-drawn motifs remain, and presently the hand-drawn element disappeared altogether, leaving only tie-dyed motifs. To create even more colorful designs, embroidery was added. And so we enter the age of *nui-shibori*—the combination of embroidery and tie-dyeing. The brevity of the life of *tsujigahana* designs was due in part to limitations inherent in the technique, but part of the

◁ *161 (opposite page, left). Detail of Noh costume* (atsuita). *Design of willow tree. Seventeenth or eighteenth century (Edo period). Itsukushima Shrine, Hiroshima Prefecture.*

◁ *162 (opposite page, right). Noh costume* (nuihaku). *Design of scattered fans and* karakusa *scrolls on red ground. Seventeenth or eighteenth century (Edo period). Shinshiro Noh Society, Aichi Prefecture.*

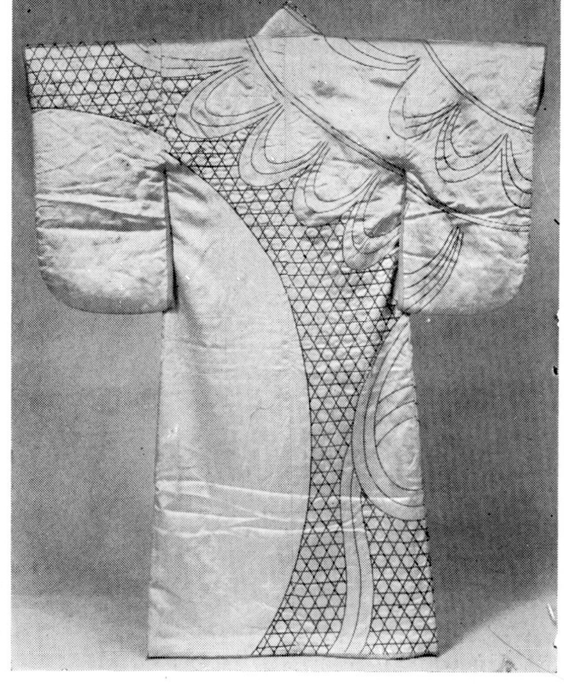

*163.* Furisode. *White satin;* nuihaku *design of basketwork and festoons of cloth. Second half of seventeenth century (mid-Edo period). Tokyo National Museum.*

blame lies also with the capricious nature of the age in which they flourished, which was always seeking new, ever more gorgeous forms of display.

Because *tsujigahana* was so short-lived, I would like to consider when and where it originated. As regards the period, a document dated 1530 has been found with some *tsujigahana* Buddhist ritual banners, recording that a monk of Negoro-ji temple donated the banners. The banners have a design of maple leaves executed in a quite advanced technique, and it is possible that the origin of *tsujigahana* goes back some fifty or sixty years earlier, to the so-called Higashiyama period. This is the time of the eighth Ashigaka shogun, Yoshimasa (r. 1449–73), and is named after the Higashiyama (Eastern Hills) outskirts of Kyoto, where he had his villa. The Higashiyama period has an importance for Japanese art out of all proportion to its short duration, the reason being that under Yoshimasa's patronage vast progress was made in many fields of art.

It is probably safe to assume that *tsujigahana* was developed in Kyoto, since this was the center of the Japanese textile industry at the time, but the particular sensibility shown in the designs and the name *tsujigahana* itself bring to mind Nara. The hand-drawn motifs, in particular, are reminiscent of the brushwork of *nara-e,* small polychrome paintings taking their subject matter from romances and similar literature and produced in large quantities in the workshops of Nara temples.

## WOVEN DESIGNS

Woven fabrics are created by the interlocking of warp and weft threads, and the way these threads are interwoven determines the style of the weave. *Aya* (twill) and *rinzu* (figured satin) are two weaves. The use of different colors for some of the warp

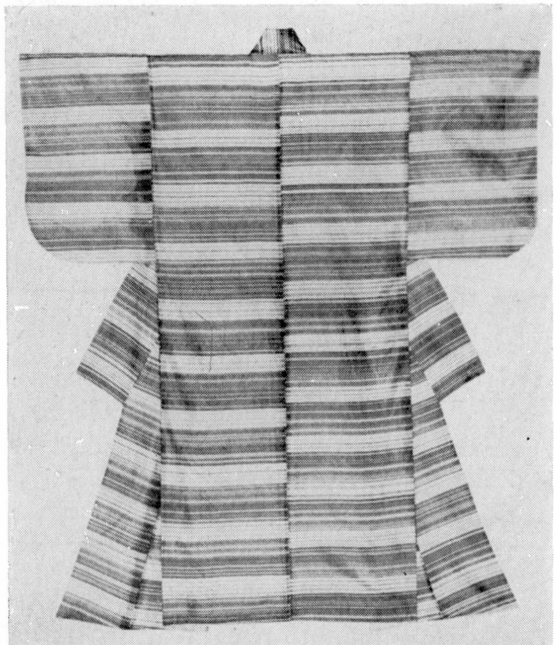

*164. Noh costume* (noshime). *Design of white, yellowish-green, and red stripes (the so-called Arihira stripes). Eighteenth or nineteenth century (Edo period). Tokugawa Art Museum, Nagoya.*

and weft threads results in a type of cloth having complicated and beautifully colored designs. These fabrics are a kind of brocade called *nishiki*. The demand for figured weaves and brocades appeared in ancient times, and the fabrics themselves are the result of the accumulation of many people's effort and experience over many years. Noh costumes and kosode made their appearance on the foundation of such weaving techniques. In turn, the development of Noh costumes and kosode provided a strong stimulus for advances in weaving techniques.

We know from extant examples that weaves like *aya, nishiki,* and *tsuzure-ori* (a type of tapestry weave) were being produced with great skill in the Nara period. Their quality dropped somewhat in the Heian period, but the tradition was not broken, and these cloths were used for garments of the nobility. However, at the court, the designs and techniques of these materials became fixed and stereotyped, and no great advances were made. The tradition can still be seen today in the so-called *yusoku* patterns.

Contact with the advanced textiles of Sung-period (960–1279) China, intercourse with which was renewed in the Kamakura period, gave a fresh impetus to this refined but stagnant world of textiles. However, in this age of government by the samurai class, whose basic creed was a life of frugality, there were few such patrons to encourage the development of textiles. In the ensuing Muromachi period, the ruling elite began to show more interest in sartorial elegance.

Toward the end of the Muromachi period, there was a renewed interest in textiles, leading to the development of advanced weaving techniques. Cities like Sakai (near modern Osaka), Hakata (northern Kyushu), and Yamaguchi (in modern Yamaguchi Prefecture), all centers of foreign trade, were stimulated by imported cloths, and perhaps foreign weavers even played a part in this sudden resurgence of textile development. It is only natural that all these techniques came together in Kyoto, the cultural center, and made famous the name of Nishijin, the center of the textile industry within Kyoto. The interest in beautiful clothes made possible by the stable conditions of the Momoyama period was an important factor in the development of Nishijin weaving techniques. But the continuing popularity of embroidery in the Momoyama period indicates that cloths with woven designs were still too expensive and weaving techniques had not reached a sufficiently high level to replace embroidery.

Japanese weaving technique reached its peak in the early Edo period. The techniques that had been carefully nurtured until then reached maturity, and important support for this development was provided by the Noh theater. Although the Noh costumes of the Momoyama period were excellent in design, technically those of the early Edo period were more advanced.

In the beginning, Chinese fabrics were highly prized for Noh costumes, so that the first task was to equal the level of Chinese textile techniques.

Secondly, female *shite* (protagonist) roles were the most important type of role in Noh, and the colorful brocaded stuff called *karaori* ("Chinese weave") and imported from China, as its name suggests, was much sought after for the costumes of these female roles. As Noh grew in popularity, it became necessary for this type of cloth to be produced in Japan. Thirdly, since Noh costumes were made specifically for theatrical purposes, it was possible to develop weaves and colorful designs without having to take into consideration their practicality. Fourthly, from the Momoyama into the Edo period, the daimyo and the Tokugawa shoguns were ardent patrons of Noh and grudged no expense for the production of costumes, thus allowing the weavers and dyers to give free rein to their imagination and skill.

Among the *karaori* and *atsuita* Noh costumes are some that are made from cloths of a stiffness that makes them quite impractical for ordinary clothing. These weaves are possible only because they are used for Noh costumes. Thus, although at first the object was to make imitations of imported Chinese materials, eventually this led to the creation of new types of purely Japanese textiles quite different from the imported cloths. *Ukimon-ori* (literally, "floating-design weave") is a good example of this. Here, relatively long lengths of the threads that form the design are "floated" on the surface without being bound to the body of the fabric. This type of weave was popular in the Heian period, when it was known as *ukisen-aya*. Because of the excellent sheen of the *ukimon* weave it is highly suitable for stage costumes; the *karaori* Noh costume of Figure 14 makes the most of this characteristic. In contrast, stiff weaves using no floating threads give the sense of mass that is another component of the beauty of Noh costumes, as can be seen from the *atsuita* shown in Figure 13. Progress in weaving during the Momoyama and early Edo periods was not restricted to figured weaves, for the striped fabrics called *noshime* and checked fabrics were also new developments of the time.

In this way weaving techniques improved rapidly under the stimulus of the Noh, but by the middle of the Edo period Noh costume had lost its aesthetic freedom as a form of stage costume due to the influence of the utilitarian kosode and to the fact that the financial resources of the daimyo were beginning to dwindle. With insufficient patronage, the technical level declined. Fortunately, however, the tradition did not die out completely and can still be seen today in the fabrics used for obi sashes.

*165. Detail of Nishijin brocade. The imaginary* hosoge *flower.*

Kyoto was the seat of the Otoneri-za (Bureau of Imperial Attendants) and of the Gofuku-dokoro, a bureau descended from the Oribe no Tsukasa (Bureau of Weaving) and charged with the supply of clothing to the court. It was perfectly natural, therefore, that Kyoto should have been the main center of the development of weaving technique. Cloth was also woven in other places but was of only ordinary quality. Only Kyoto could produce truly high-quality textiles. At the beginning of the Onin civil war (1467–77) the majority of weavers left

*166. Detail of Tenjukoku Embroidered Mandala. Silk; first half of seventh century. Chugu-ji, Nara.*

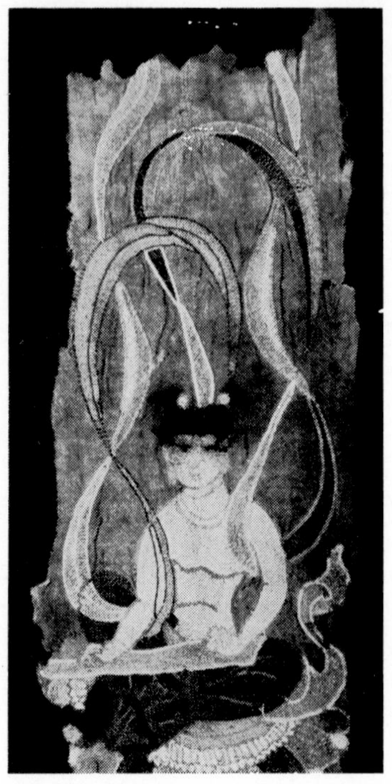

*167. Fragment of embroidered Buddhist banner showing flying angel. Eighth century. Tokyo National Museum.*

Kyoto in search of powerful patrons in the flourishing provincial towns. But when the fighting was over, the weavers returned and settled in what had been the camp of the so-called western faction during the disturbances—the present Nishijin (literally, "western camp"). This now became one of the centers of the weaving industry. Eventually the weavers of Nishijin formed a strong guild and were able to maintain their own special characteristics in the face of changing tastes and conditions. Many Nishijin weavers worked for a particular patronage; some wove for the court, some for daimyo, some for Shinto shrines, some for Buddhist temples, and some for the Noh schools. The fact that *noshime* striped-fabric weavers exercised considerable authority among them tells us to what a great extent *noshime* stripes had struck the fancy of the age.

EMBROIDERY Embroidery also has a long history. Before the techniques of woven or even dyed designs were known, the art of embroidery made possible the decoration of cloth. Even among primitive peoples, embroidered decoration has been known from early times. One advantage that embroidery has over woven designs is that of flexibility. To make woven designs feasible, quantity production is a necessity, since a certain amount of time is required to set up a loom for a given design. Embroidery, on the other hand, involving no mechanical equipment, imposes no such condition, and designs can be freely varied. Furthermore, for practical purposes the only limitation on the kinds of designs that can be executed in embroidery is the colors made available by the dyers. The technique of weaving, on the other hand, is complicated, and there are a great number of limitations on the kinds of designs that can be realized.

Embroidery shares something of the freedom and flexibility of painting, and has the advantage of being more striking than painting. For this reason, even in times when painting methods were advanced, for large picture areas the beauty of embroidered colors was preferred to paints. In Japan, embroidered mandalas were made from an early time, among them the Tenjukoku Mandala (Fig. 166) of the Chugu-ji nunnery at the Horyu-ji, and many different embroidery stitches were known. Embroidery was also used for the clothing of the aristocracy in the Nara and Heian periods.

Embroidery was particularly popular during the Muromachi and Momoyama periods. Many garments from these periods, whether Noh costumes or kosode, were entirely covered with embroidery (Fig. 72). We may surmise that neither the art of weaving nor that of dyeing was as yet very versatile. Even when these techniques became more sophisticated, embroidery remained highly popular. The "floating thread" designs of *ukimon-ori* were probably an attempt to reproduce the effect of embroidery. In other woven and dyed designs, the makers were obliged to use some embroidery to add highlights to the design. This tradition is still to be seen in Japanese costume today.

*168. Detail of kosode material. White figured satin; design of maple leaves in* hitta-kanoko *tie-dyed spots and embroidery. Eighteenth century (Edo period).*

In Muromachi and Momoyama times the dyeing and weaving industries were functioning on a cottage-industry basis. Woven and dyed designs were not entirely satisfactory, and embroidery was very popular. Edo-period embroidery presumably developed from that of Muromachi and Momoyama times. The technique was used not only to decorate clothes but also to make Buddhist images. But on comparing the embroidery of the Buddhist images and that of clothing, we find that although the Buddhist embroideries were made by devotees and are intricate works, there is something faltering and clumsy about them. Costume embroidery, on the other hand, may seem sketchy but suggests a practiced hand. It is in costumes that the unique beauty of Japanese embroidery is found. From the Sung to the Ming period, Chinese embroidery also showed delicate and elaborate workmanship, but it somehow seems stiff and cold compared to the warmth of Japanese work. From the mid-Edo period onward, Japanese embroidery techniques multiplied and workmanship became neat and accurate. Ironically, however, this led to the loss of the powerful effect of Japanese embroidery.

Basically, the beauty of embroidery lies in the fact that it brings a feeling of depth to what would otherwise be flat areas of color. For this reason roughness of texture is an important quality, and the work of the Muromachi and Momoyama periods made full use of this characteristic (Fig. 9). Seen in this light, the work of the mid-Edo period and later seems to have lost sight of the basic beauty of embroidery through an undue emphasis on technique. On the other hand, the skill and intricacy of this work would have been impossible in any other period, and the unflagging patience to

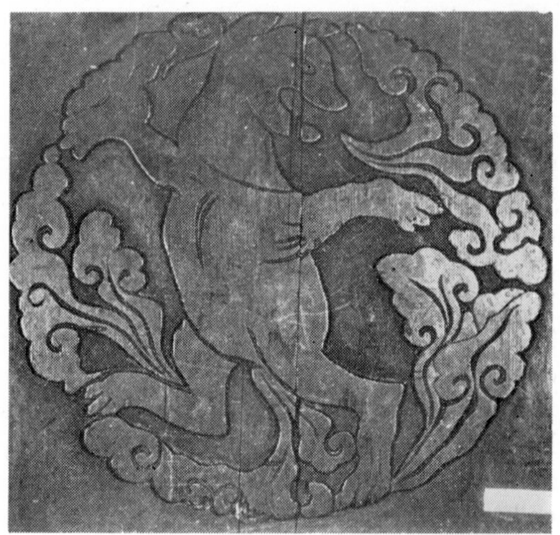

which it bears witness should receive due recognition.

DYEING AND PRINTING

Improved dyeing techniques also had an effect on costumes. Although the decoration of textiles by dyeing is a simpler process than either weaving or embroidery, dyed designs lack a sense of mass or weight. And because such fabrics were used mainly for the clothes of the lower classes, dyeing techniques were late in developing. In the Nara period *kokechi* (tie-dyeing), *rokechi* (wax-resist dyeing), and *kyokechi* (block-resist dyeing) were known. In the succeeding Heian period tie-dyeing is known to have been still in use, but the fate of wax-resist and block-resist dyeing is unclear. Stencil dyeing and block printing, both of which could be described as a cross between the wax-resist and block-resist methods, were the only techniques developed to an advanced stage in the Heian period.

The Japanese term *kata-zome* includes both stencil dyeing and printing from blocks, and primitive forms of both were used in the Nara period. The so-called *ban-e* designs (Fig. 170) and decorated writing paper are Heian-period examples of block printing. As economical, large-scale production was possible with these methods, their use was widespread. Eventually stencil-dyeing was made easier by replacing the wooden stencils used hitherto with ones made from thick paper. Another development was the addition of resist-dyeing methods to the stencil-dyeing repertory. Thus, instead of dyes being applied to the cloth through the cut-out parts of the stencil, dye-repellent substances like wax or rice paste were applied, so that those parts were reserved from the dye and remained the natural color of the cloth. We know that at the end of the Heian period and in the Kamakura period, leather armor fittings were dyed by this method; so costume textiles were probably also being decorated by this process. Some of the garments worn by lowly figures represented in picture scrolls of the time seem to be decorated with designs that could only have been produced with these methods. The stiff sleeveless jackets called *kataginu,* used in Kyogen for such roles as those of servants, are thought to represent a continuation of this tradition.

◁ *169 (opposite page, left). Detail of Noh costume* (nuihaku) *showing embroidered clematis scrolls on black ground. Seventeenth century (early Edo period.) Tokyo National Museum.*

◁ *170 (opposite page, right). Woodblock of* ban-e *medallion design; bear and flames.*

*171. Detail of kosode. Gray crepe; "shaded" dyed design of landscape with towed boats. Eighteenth or nineteenth century (late Edo period).*

Once paper started to be used for stencils instead of wood, the cutting of stencils became a much simpler operation. Small, delicate designs became possible, and so the *komon* ("small pattern") designs were born. These are designs made by the repetition of small motifs (Fig. 173). That both the *dofuku* of Tokugawa Ieyasu and the *kataginu* costumes of Kyogen included some with *komon* designs indicates their popularity at the time. *Komon* patterns attained a subdued beauty, but they became so delicate that their expressiveness was weakened, so that in reaction coarser, medium-sized patterns were developed. These can still be seen today in the cloths used for the light cotton summer kimono called *yukata*.

## CHAYA-ZOME AND YUZEN

Among the various stencil and block processes, the *chaya-zome* method, named after a Kyoto draper called Chaya Shirojiro, is outstanding. Chaya Shirojiro was an early Edo-period supplier of specially dyed material to high-ranking samurai women for summer garments of a type called *katabira*. This material was made from well-bleached high-quality hemp, and was dyed by the careful application of paste on both sides of the cloth to the parts to be reserved from the dye, thus producing an evenly dyed fabric of very high quality (Figs. 111, 172).

*Yuzen-zome* is a method resembling *chaya-zome* but is free from the restrictions imposed by the use of stencils. This freedom of design made a lively contribution to the costumes of the Edo period. The *yuzen-zome* process is said to have been invented in the early part of the Edo period by the painter Miyazaki Yuzensai. The process consists in painting a design on the cloth with paints and dyestuffs, fixing this with a liquor made from beans, and covering the design with rice paste, after which the background is dyed by immersion in dye liquor. This method has the advantage of making possible detailed pictorial designs. However, since the *komon* process utilizing stencils and paste resist was already known, such a process alone would not have been enough to make *yuzen* famous. I think this type of textile was named after Yuzensai because, being a painter, he used pictorial designs in contrast with the pattern type of design used until then.

*172 (far left). Detail of* katabira *material. White hemp;* chaya-zome *dyed design of landscape with chirping-insect cage. Eighteenth century (Edo period).*

*173 (left). Detail of kosode material.* Komon *allover design of cherry blossoms. Eighteenth century (Edo period).*

*174. Detail of* furisode. *Kaga* yuzen *dyed design of flower baskets. Eighteenth century (Edo period).*

*Yuzen* came to specialize in pictorial designs and developed shading and similar techniques in order to emphasize the hand-painted nature of its designs. But the closer *yuzen* designs approached the quality of real painting, the more they lost the unique beauty of dyed designs. There are several examples of hanging picture scrolls that are actually *yuzen* dyed fabrics—not only the picture itself but also the cloth borders that usually form part of the mounting are dyed on a single piece of cloth. Many of these are traditionally attributed to Yuzensai himself. They are interesting attempts, but they are presumptuous in trespassing on the territory of painting proper. *Yuzen-zome* had to pay the price for this arrogance. However close to the effect of real painting it came, it could never surpass it. Actually, *yuzen* fabrics should have had a special beauty not to be seen in paintings. But it was some time before this was realized.

Apart from the *yuzen-zome* that grew up around Kyoto, another *yuzen* tradition developed at Kanazawa in Kaga Province, present Ishikawa Prefecture (Figs. 132, 174). It is considered a subtradition of the one in Kyoto. Some say that Yuzensai moved to Kaga, but there is no firm evidence for this. One thing is certain: the two forms of *yuzen* influenced each other. Kaga *yuzen* uses brighter colors than Kyoto *yuzen* and is often thought to be more charming. But neither tradition was fully aware of the true potential of the process and for a long time both vied to win favor with women. Such favor gave *yuzen* its fame, but basically it worked against the optimum development of the art. That is why so few examples of *yuzen* fabrics are discussed in this book. In fact, even when *yuzen* was in its prime it was not used in Noh costumes because it had a fundamentally different kind of beauty from that of Noh, and the discerning Noh performers realized this.

## KIRIHAME AND ZOGAN

The term *kirihame* includes both appliqué and patchwork. The kind of *katami-gawari* design made by putting together pieces of two different cloths for the left and right halves of a kimono could be said to be an example of this method. *Katami-gawari* kimono were sometimes made for economy reasons, but the true purpose of *kirihame* is to achieve a complex effect by combining several simpler designs. The idea is similar to that of the paper collages of the *Sanjuroku-nin Kashu* anthology (Fig. 120). Examples of a similar effect, although achieved by different methods, can be seen in what I called composite designs (Figs. 34, 101), in the Temmon kosode (Figs. 35, 123), and in the *furisode* of Figures 6 and 112. The Temmon kosode is a patchwork of some six different kinds of design, while the *furisode* is made up of about fifteen different kinds. The individual designs are such that a harmonious effect is achieved. Some Noh costumes and kosode use two or three kinds of pattern in seemingly casual but attractive designs of this type.

The *kirihame* method, however, was not invented in the Edo period. The tradition stretches back to the Heian period, when it was known as *zogan,* a term now generally used to refer to inlay in metalwork, woodwork, and ceramics. In an account of a New Year's poetry competition at the empress's residence in 1056, the *Eiga Monogatari* describes the clothes of those present. One garment is described as having a blue *zogan* design on a white ground. Since there are also records of the use of mother-of-pearl, gold-dust lacquer work (*maki-e*), and strung beads for costume decoration, the use of *kirihame* is not very surprising. Kabuki costumes of the late Edo period, as they became increasingly bizarre, approached this decorative profusion, but fortunately the *kirihame* of Edo period kosode never reached that stage.

## HAND-PAINTED DESIGNS

The drawing or painting of a design directly on cloth is one of the most primitive and simplest methods of textile decoration and has been used since earliest times. We have a number of examples from the Nara period preserved in the Shoso-in repository. They include scroll designs in Chinese ink and vermilion floral lozenges. The tradition continued in the Heian period, when it was customary for the skirts worn by noblewomen to have hand-painted pictorial designs in gold and silver pigments. The *Eiga Monogatari* mentions

*175. Kyogen costume* (kataginu). *Stencil-dyed design of hydrangea blossoms and butterflies. Eighteenth century (Edo period).*

*176 (opposite page, left). Kyogen costume* (kataginu). *Dyed design of loquats on a brown ground and yellowish-green triangular-scale motifs. Seventeenth or eighteenth century (Edo period). Itsukushima Shrine, Hiroshima Prefecture.* ▷

*177 (opposite page, right). Kyogen costume* (kataginu). *Design of hares and mare's-tails. Seventeenth or eighteenth century (Edo period).* ▷

hand-painted designs in describing the clothes worn in 1030 at a cherry-blossom-viewing party and at the Kamo festival in Kyoto.

We know from the *Kasuga Miracles* picture scroll that the servants of Kamakura-period samurai wore *kariginu* robes with hand-painted designs. I mentioned earlier that the *kataginu* costumes used in Kyogen represent a continuation of this tradition. And the development of *tsujigahana* designs was possible because of this tradition of hand-painted decoration. The famous decorative painter Ogata Korin undertook the design of kimono (Figs. 5, 87) at the end of the seventeenth century because such a tradition was in existence, and the Kabuki character Gosho no Gorozo in the play of the same name, first performed in 1864, is made to commission a famous painter of the time to do an ink-monochrome painting because of the general liking for pictorial designs. The fact that this primitive, simple technique survived in the most elaborate and sophisticated designs was perhaps a reaction to the impersonality of mass-production methods and indicates a search for a more human touch.

## COLORS AND THEIR NAMES

Although form and design are also important elements, the beauty of many Noh costumes and kosode lies in their color. The colors used depended in part on functional considerations, but also, of course, on taste, which changed with the passage of time. In order to know what colors were used, we need to have either the actual garments or color photographs of them. But even if we have the actual garments, some colors, such as red, tend to fade considerably, so it is difficult to tell what the original colors were. We have old records of colors, but the names appearing in them are not much help in determining the exact colors used.

Many colors have special names peculiar to the

textile industry. Some traditional color names survive, while others have died out. Color names like *moegi* (yellowish green) and *nando* (grayish blue), for example, present no problem to women, who still use these terms in the context of fashion today. But men are not so familiar with them. And there are many color terms that will put even women at a loss. In order to avoid the instability and inaccuracy of traditional color terminology, attempts have been made to establish a set of standard colors and label them with numbers. From a practical point of view this is convenient, but it seems unfortunate that a world of color has turned into one of numbers. We can see a kind of cultural history of color in the endless process of color terms coming into use and dying out.

The total range of colors is a continuum, and different cultures subdivide this continuum in different ways. If we look at the history of Japanese terminology, we find that at first only simple distinctions were made. Greater sophistication was achieved when Chinese color terms were introduced, and from the Asuka to the Heian period, the Japanese made color distinctions according to Chinese terminology. At first the colors distinguished were the simple *murasaki* (purple), *ao* (blue and green), *aka* (red), *ki* (yellow), *shiro* (white), and *kuro* (black), and they were qualified as being deep or shallow (dark or light). These are the colors for the costumes of various ranks of courtiers as fixed in the time of Empress Suiko (r. 592–628). But by the Nara period the court colors had become somewhat more complicated and *hi* (scarlet), *kon* (a deep, navy-blue shade of indigo), and *midori* (a shade of green) had been added. *Ai* (a dark-blue shade of indigo), *heki* (a green), *suo* (a dark red), and *hanada* (a shade of indigo lighter than *ai*) are some of the other terms that began to be used. Thus it had become necessary to make fine color distinctions. It was no longer satisfactory to qualify

*178. Detail of Noh-costume fabric* (atsuita). *Design of stylized chrysanthemum blossoms on* yamagata *("mountain forms") zigzag ground. Sixteenth or seventeenth century (Muromachi or Momoyama period).*

*179. Detail of Noh costume* (nuihaku). *Design of "snowflake ring" medallions and dandelions. Seventeenth century (mid-Edo period). Tokugawa Art Museum, Nagoya.*

colors simply as deep or light—subtle terms like *aokatsu* (a dark brown with a tinge of blue) and *messhi* (a slightly faded purple) were introduced.

In the Heian period, further distinctions of hue became necessary, and names of flowers, grasses, and birds were adopted to widen the scope of color terminology. *Ebi* (shrimp) for a reddish brown, *kuchiha* (decaying leaves) for a reddish yellow, *yamabuki* (kerria rose) for a deep yellow, and *shion* (aster) for a light purple are examples of such color names. These names were still used by courtiers in the Kamakura period and even later. They influenced the language of society at large, too, but it is doubtful whether commoners were as sensitive to the nuances of color as were the court nobles. On the contrary, it seems that commoners considered these subtle color distinctions a bother and made do with a simplified terminology in their everyday lives.

Colors distinguished during the Muromachi period included *murasaki* (purple), *aka* (red), *beni* (red), *ao* (blue and green), *moegi* (yellowish green), *asagi* (light blue), *ki* (yellow), *cha* (brown), *kon* (navy blue), *nezumi* (gray), *tobi-iro* (dark brown), *ukon-iro* (yellow), and *kaki-iro* (persimmon). Brown and gray, in particular, were finely subdivided into numerous shades. But the growing fondness for bright and extravagant clothes could not be satisfied by these alone. In an age that gave itself up to the pursuit of fashion, any new name for a color was welcome, even when the color itself was the same.

Textiles made around the Nara period display a clear, striking beauty in their skillful combination of a small number of colors. It is true that high-quality textiles of the time include some, such as those preserved in the Shoso-in in Nara, that display complex and subtle color combinations, but on the whole the demand was for clarity.

These lines from a poem in the eighth-century anthology *Man'yo-shu* describe the clear-cut costume colors that were popular in those days:

> Over the great vermilion-painted bridge
>   across Katashiwa River
> Hem of crimson skirt trailing
> Wearing a robe dyed with mountain indigo
> A girl walks alone. . . .

But Heian nobles, in their pursuit of elegance, preferred colors that softly blended with each other to the powerful contrasts described above. For example, rather than sharp contrasts between the

*180. Detail of Noh costume* (atsuita). *Design of wisterias and braided fence. Seventeenth or eighteenth century (Edo period). Tokugawa Art Museum, Nagoya.*

*181. Detail of Noh costume* (choken). *Design of grasses woven in gold thread on* sayagata *ground pattern. Seventeenth or eighteenth century (Edo period). Tokugawa Art Museum, Nagoya.*

colors of the outside and the lining of a robe, or between top and bottom, a gradual change of hue, either continuous or in stages, was favored. The *kasane no irome* (color combinations of layered robes), known by such names as *kobai* (red plum), *sakura* (cherry), *yamabuki* (kerria rose), *unohana* (*Deutzia crenata*), *fuji* (wisteria), *ominaeshi* (*Patrinia scabiosaefolia*), and *kuchiha* (decaying leaves) are a manifestation of the desire for harmonious beauty. The popularity at the time of colors that shaded into each other in dyed cloths like *murago* and *suego* was also due to the desire for softness in colors. The word *nioi* was frequently used to express beauty in the Heian period. The original meaning of this word was something like "effulgence" or "glow," and the term suggests colors emitting an aura into the atmosphere. The aristocrats of the Heian period captured this effulgent, glowing quality by making colors bright and blending them gradually. The same preference for gradual change is the reason a shade of gray called *usu-nibi-iro* was worn for mourning rather than black. It represented not a sudden descent into the dark of night but a gradual transition into twilight.

The Japanese of the Kamakura period lost this fine sensitivity to color. The glowing quality of colors and their bright warmth disappeared. Although there are no extant garments to show this, it is apparent from the colors used in paintings of the period and from costumes shown in genre paintings. In the Muromachi period, when Noh costumes were assuming their definitive form, a new feeling for color appeared in contrast to the concept of *nioi* in the Nara and Heian periods. This was the subdued, severe beauty referred to as *shibui*. (The literal meaning of this term is "astringent.") This development was greatly influenced by the coloring of Chinese textiles. In the Sung period the Chinese abandoned the sumptuous, colorful taste of T'ang times and sought a more profound refinement. Later this was to become the quality known as *shibusa* ("astringency") in Japanese. It can be seen in the imported cloths called *meibutsu-gire,* in which primary colors are avoided as much as possible. Eventually the aesthetic ideals of *wabi* and *sabi* developed out of the concept of *shibusa*.

However, the popular color sense of the Momoyama period made full enjoyment of these refined colors impossible. Once more we see the bold smashing of tradition. Bright, startling color combinations came to life again. A new beauty of color, based on a peculiar combination of re-

*182. Detail of Noh costume* (atsuita). *Design of tortoise-shell motifs, crane lozenges, and chrysanthemum lozenges. Seventeenth or eighteenth century (Edo period). Tokugawa Art Museum, Nagoya.*

*183 (opposite page, left). Detail of Noh costume* (atsuita). *Check design. Seventeenth or eighteenth century (Edo period). Noda Shrine, Yamaguchi Prefecture.* ▷

*184 (opposite page, right). Detail of Noh costume* (kariginu). *Gold brocade; Buddhist wheel motifs on a ground of* tatewaku *undulating lines. Seventeenth or eighteenth century (Edo period). Tokugawa Art Museum, Nagoya.* ▷

strained and flamboyant colors, came into being. This strong contrast was partly softened by *surihaku* and *shibori-zome.* The distinctive characteristic of Momoyama costume colors is this blending of restraint and boldness.

In the first part of the Edo period costumes were becoming increasingly showy, and although in general the tendencies of the Momoyama period can be said to have continued, both the subdued and the bold elements weakened, and there was an indiscriminate admixture of color preferences of earlier times. This was the age of the rise of merchant-class culture, and although its color sense is only a superficial imitation of the older color ideals, there is a kind of bold, rich beauty about it. We might liken it to a stew in country cooking. As techniques and materials improved, this country "crudeness" gradually came to display an attractive color sense. The high regard in which early-Edo Noh costumes and kosode are held today is also due to this.

However, we cannot deny that there is something jumbled about the colors. A tendency to simplify and create order appeared. The trendsetters were actors, courtesans, and tea-ceremony masters. Their taste is represented by such aesthetic ideals as *datè, iki,* and *shibusa.* In the costumes of the late Edo period, tastes separated and went their various ways. Here and there we see a refined sense of color, but overall it is a hodgepodge.

ABSTRACT MOTIFS Many interesting motifs are used in kosode and Noh costume designs. Although motifs were seemingly invented in an endless stream, to create one new motif after another is in fact difficult, and there are many that have been repeated several times.

The abstract patterns on Noh costumes and kosode consist of arrangements of straight lines and curves. Figurative patterns represent such things as flowers and birds. Let us look first of all at abstract motifs consisting of straight lines only. There are the vertical trellis (*koshi;* Fig. 183), the diagonal trellis (*tasuki*), the basket design (*kagome,* consisting of horizontal and diagonal lines), and braided cypress fencing (*higaki,* consisting of diagonal lines). Because of the simplicity of these motifs, their range of application is wide, and they have been in use for a long time. Examples of complex combinations of straight lines are lightning (*rai*), tortoise shell (*kikko*), joined swastikas (*manji-tsunagi*), and the so-called *saya* pattern (*saya-gata*), thought to be derived from the joined swastikas and so named because variants of this motif are traditionally used

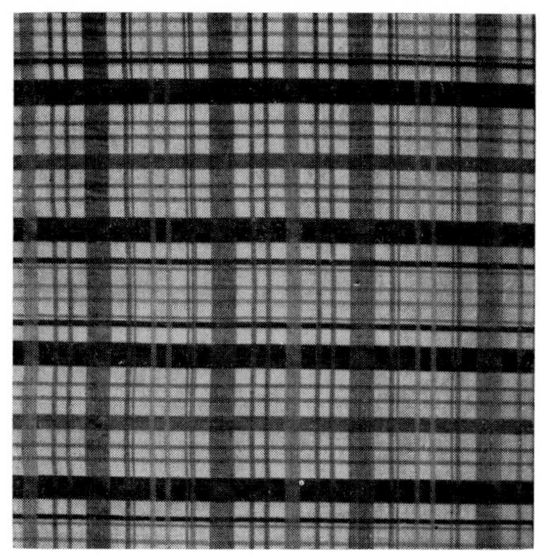

as the ground design on a type of figured satin called *saya.* (This design can be seen clearly on the kosode of Figure 20 and the *furisode* of Figure 33.) These more complex motifs have been used in China since ancient times, and the lightning and joined-swastika designs were incorporated into Buddhist art at an early period.

The firm stability of the joined hexagons of the tortoise-shell motif makes it ideal as an expression of commanding dignity. Sometimes, in order to soften the effect a little, a stylized floral pattern called *karahana* (literally, "Chinese flower") is placed in the hexagons. The *saya* design was introduced into Japan on Ming textiles, and originally had an exotic attraction for the Japanese. There is a smart, *iki* feeling about this variation on the joined swastikas, and it was a favorite pattern on Edo-period kosode. Even today it has its staunch admirers. The "joined hemp-leaves" (*asanoha-tsunagi;* Fig. 188) is another Chinese motif associated with Buddhism. Like the *saya,* this design was much used on Edo-period kosode, perhaps because the hemp leaf has feminine associations in Japan and because the design is a very delicate one with clearly visible diagonal lines. When executed in tie-dyed textiles, the effect is truly bewitching.

Similar are the lozenge or diamond motifs (*hishigata*). The "pine-bark lozenge" (*matsukawa-bishi*), popular throughout the Muromachi and Momoyama periods, belongs to this group. It does not actually represent pine bark, but the name seems to give it poetic overtones. Giving figurative motifs a more or less lozenge-shaped outline helps to soften them and imparts a feeling of *iki.* Examples of this are the crane lozenge (*tsuru-bishi;* Fig. 182), consisting of two cranes with spread wings, and the pine lozenge (*matsu-bishi*), similarly made up of two pines. There is also the *kiku-bishi,* in which the normally round chrysanthemum blossom is distorted into a lozenge shape (Fig. 182).

In contrast with these rectilinear designs there are some consisting primarily of curved lines. Representative of these is *shippo-tsunagi,* consisting of interlocking rings (Fig. 191). This motif has a long tradition, having been often used in Buddhist art since the Heian period. Its frequent use on Noh costumes and kosode is due to the fact that the meaning of the word *shippo* (seven treasures) is auspicious. But the regular curves of this pattern are liable to be felt as too tranquil, and there is a tendency for the motif to become *yabo,* or unimaginative. *Tatewaku* ("vertical seething"; Fig. 184) is another curvilinear design, but in their opposed undulation the lines alternately approach each

*185. Detail of Noh costume* (karaori). *Design of autumn plants on a braided-fence ground. Seventeenth or eighteenth century (Edo period). Tokugawa Art Museum, Nagoya.*

*186 (opposite page, left). Detail of Noh costume* (atsuita). *Design of swastika and scudding clouds. Seventeenth or eighteenth century (Edo period). Tokugawa Art Museum, Nagoya.* ▷

*187 (opposite page, right). Detail of Noh costume* (karaori). *Design of chrysanthemums on ground of chessboard checks. Seventeenth or eighteenth century (Edo period). Tokugawa Art Museum, Nagoya.* ▷

other and separate, thus creating a sense of movement. The *tatewaku* also has a long history. In the Heian period it was sometimes used on its own but also in combination with clouds, scrolls, or wisteria blossoms. When the spaces between the swinging lines are covered, the effect of light suppleness characteristic of *tatewaku* is diminished. In this respect the *nuihaku* Noh costume of Figure 114 is especially fine. Although it uses *tatewaku* as a ground, the design is not constricted by this, and the lily motifs are freely distributed. There is a strong suggestion of the expansive, unfettered mood of the Momoyama period.

Among circular designs there is a group called *yo-mon.* These originally represented constellations and typically consist of a number of roundels or filled circles surrounding a larger one. The *shichiyo-mon* (seven circles) and *kuyo-mon* (nine circles; Foldout 2) are common examples. Their origin goes back to Persia, and they have been in use in Japan since the Nara period. Although they appear on Noh costumes, they were not used on kosode, perhaps because they were too lacking in variety. Instead, family-crest designs consisting of combinations of different round motifs and floral medallions consisting of grasses and flowers with a circular outline were used on kosode. The medallions were scattered asymmetrically in order to alleviate the monotonous effect of so many circles.

There are various ways of distributing the motifs of a design. Two typical ways are the scattered and the dense arrangements. The dense type of arrangement gives a bright, colorful effect and was popular in T'ang-period China and Nara-period Japan. The "floating-thread" designs called *ukisen-aya* of the Heian period belong to the same tradition. However, although these were excellent designs, they resembled the classical ones too much, so that attempts were made to devise ways to break their severity and give a feeling of freedom. The floral medallions were examples of this. So were the butterfly medallions, which were a way of giving variety to the butterfly shape. This type of design partakes of the nature of both abstract and figurative designs. Thus although motifs can be roughly classified into abstract and figurative categories, designs often incorporate elements of both types.

FIGURATIVE MOTIFS Figurative designs are characterized by greater freedom than abstract ones. On the whole, abstract motifs give a somewhat serious and solemn impression, suitable for Noh costumes, while figurative motifs have a rather lighter, more relaxed feeling

and were preferred for kosode. I want to examine here not their composition but rather the subjects chosen for representation. Most popular, as might be expected, are flowers, since these emphasize feminine grace. Blossoms most commonly found on textiles are the plum, cherry, wisteria, and bush clover. Since early times, these have been treated in poetry and have strong and profound poetic associations. Because of this and because they were employed frequently, great pains were taken with their treatment on textiles. From the Momoyama to the early Edo period, the hydrangea increased in popularity as a subject of figurative designs. However, because its blossoms tend to fade quickly—it is considered to be symbolic of the transience of life—the hydrangea is superstitiously avoided in modern designs. Its use in the Momoyama and Edo periods was no doubt due to its novelty as a design and to its beautiful purple color (although it has other colors too; Figs. 63, 103). The lotus, symbolic of purity, has been used so much in Buddhist contexts that it is almost never found either on Noh costumes or on kosode. It would seem that the motif was avoided because it was too redolent of religion.

Apart from blossoms, such subjects as tree trunks and leaves also appeared as textile decoration. Very common among these were the pine, bamboo, willow, and vines. In the beginning of the Edo period, the "three companions" (pine, bamboo, and plum) and the "four gentlemen" (plum, chrysanthemum, *ran* orchid, and bamboo), both combinations symbolic of such Confucian virtues as fortitude and rectitude, became common designs. It is well known that the pine, bamboo, plum, chrysanthemum, and orchid were auspicious symbols. *Sasa* (bamboo grass) was also popular. Vines and other climbing plants often decorated the kosode of courtesans from the pleasure districts, perhaps because the image of a vine clinging to a great tree was felt to suggest femininity. The *tessenka* (clematis) is one example of this type of motif, all the more popular because of its purple blossoms. Women's costumes in paintings by Kaigetsudo Ando are often adorned with this flower.

Such plants as the chrysanthemum, iris, lily, and the so-called autumn grasses appeal to the Japanese poetic sensibility, and subjects like a chrysanthemum by a brushwood fence or irises at the water's edge have long been popular. For this reason great efforts were made to bring a touch of novelty to these motifs. However, flowers that had been used in designs for so long were inevitably felt to be trite, and so efforts were made to use new kinds

*188. Detail of kosode material. Block-resist dyed hemp-leaf pattern with embroidered characters. Eighteenth or nineteenth century (late Edo period).*

*189. Detail of Noh costume* (nuihaku). *Design of maple leaves on ground pattern of stylized waves* (seigaiha). *Eighteenth or nineteenth century (second half of Edo period). Tokugawa Art Museum, Nagoya.*

like the dandelion and the narcissus, but because the tradition behind these was shallow, there was a lack of refinement in such designs.

Even though figurative motifs are free and realistic in nature, because they are decorative it is necessary to simplify and stylize the subjects to a certain extent. But the continual search for new subjects, and particularly the popularity of realistic treatments made possible by advances in the *yuzen* method, caused efforts to simplify and stylize subject matter to be neglected.

Among animal motifs, phoenixes, cranes, *onagadori* (roosters with long tails), mandarin ducks, and plovers have long been used as auspicious symbols, and this tradition is preserved in Noh costumes and kosode. Many of these stylized designs have considerable charm. In the Muromachi period, the desire for novelty brought herons, cormorants, sparrows, swallows, and quails into the repertory. Their attraction must have been their distinctive shapes. When we enter the Edo period, hawks, eagles, and other birds of prey symbolizing power appear as part of the "dandyistic" taste of the time and were used even on women's kosode. As the effect of these motifs is not very feminine, the aim may have been to startle people. There were also charming butterfly and dragonfly designs. These too were considered auspicious. Rather different is the hare. What made this subject interesting to people seems to have been the characteristic outline of the hare with its long ears, for the older the example of this motif, the longer the ears. One kosode owned by Tokugawa Ieyasu has a "hare and waves" design. In this case the hare is used not only for the intrinsic interest of its form but also as an allusion to a legend associated with the Great Shrine at Izumo, according to which a hare crossed from the island of Oki to the province of Izumo (present Shimane Prefecture) on the mainland by running over the backs of crocodiles. Its association with such a legend gives the design a significance beyond the purely aesthetic. New motifs, though

*190. Detail of kosode. Yellow crepe;* yuzen *dyed design of falcon with maple sprigs. Late seventeenth century (first half of Edo period). Nagao Art Museum, Tokyo.*

*191. Detail of Noh costume* (karaori). *Design of maple leaves on a ground of interlocking circles. Seventeenth or eighteenth century (Edo period). Tokugawa Art Museum, Nagoya.*

they may have novelty, suffer from the disadvantage of not having such a tradition behind them.

Various utensils constitute an interesting category of design subjects. In China, the "precious things" type of design, consisting of combinations of such auspicious motifs as the so-called sacred jewels and purses, had long been used, but in Japan utensils were treated more freely. The aim was to give a touch of elegance to clothes, and many of the designs feature nature and what might be called "classical taste." Designs like *katawa-guruma* (half-cartwheels, Fig. 74; this often takes the form of "cartwheels in a stream," when only part of each wheel is visible, the other part being submerged), courtiers' carriages (Fig. 114), and folding fans had been popular with the aristocracy since early times. Objects associated with literature and calligraphy, such as *shikishi* (square poem cards), *tanzaku* (oblong poem cards), correspondence boxes, and scrolls, together with musical instruments (such as flutes, koto, and drums), illustrated aristocratic pastimes. They were loved by both those who practiced these accomplishments and those who did not. These were suitable designs for kosode, but as I mentioned earlier, motifs symbolic of power and those with mystical overtones, such as the "wheel treasure" (*rimbo,* a Buddhist symbol), conch trumpet (associated with the Shugendo sect of mountain ascetics), and *umban* ("cloud board"; a bronze plate in the shape of a stylized cloud, used as a gong in Zen monasteries), were used in the decoration of Noh costumes.

The most typically Japanese characteristic of figurative designs is the representation of natural scenery. This trait was connected with the fashion for pictorial designs and indicates how closely the Japanese identified themselves with nature. Moreover, natural motifs were not used indiscriminately. Preference was given to those that had poetic associations by virtue of their having been treated in poetry and in song—an instance of the power of tradition. Examples of this type can be seen in such designs as *ajiro* and *jakago* (two types of bamboo basketwork used in the construction of embankments), drying nets, boats, bridges, farmhouses, pavilions, and wattle and brushwood fences. The most popular were water motifs. *Suhama* (stylized sandbars), flowing water, waves, and waterfalls are some of the forms water-associated designs take. They were originally used to give a sense of the refreshing and enriching powers of water and of fluid motion, and the use of a powerful symbol like the waterfall is comparable to the inclusion of birds of prey among animal subjects.

Among motifs drawn from nature are atmospheric ones like clouds, mist, and snow. Clouds have long served as auspicious symbols, but they are sometimes used as a kind of labor-saving device in pictorial designs. In such cases they cover up part of the design so that no details need to be indicated there, in the manner of some screen paintings of Kyoto scenes. Mist is used in a similar way. Snow is perhaps the most important of these subjects, and from the Momoyama period onward, designs of snow-laden plants—such as pines, willows, and bamboo grass—were popular. One motif, the *yukiwa* (snowflake ring; Fig. 179), symbolizes snow itself. The snow-laden forms of these plants constitute, so to speak, winter versions of the design. This tendency to distinguish between seasons is no doubt a reflection of the clearly demarcated seasons characteristic of the Japanese climate.

Another typically Japanese type of design is that utilizing characters. Characters or letters were used in textile and leather decoration in other countries too, but nowhere as freely as in Japan. This tradition goes back to the Nara and Heian periods, when a form of painting called *uta-e* or *ashide-e* was practiced. In this, characters were made to blend in with natural scenery. Scattered characters were also used in costume designs of the period. Usually old, well-known poems were chosen. There are many paintings from around the beginning of the seventeenth century, however, in which the *yuna* (bathhouse girls) are shown advertising their trade by wearing robes with a scattered-character design using an ideogram meaning "to wash, to bathe." We cannot help admiring the boldness of this design.

IN THIS SECTION I have only been able to consider a few representative designs used in Noh costumes and kosode. Properly speaking, we should consider them in conjunction with motifs used in other fields in the same period—*maki-e* lacquerware, sword guards, and ceramics. With the Edo period we enter an age that willingly broke traditions in its pursuit of freedom in design. Nevertheless, the search for freedom was not an undisciplined one. Although at first sight a multitude of motifs appear to have been used, many are in fact revivals of earlier designs. A novel and unusual idea may attract people's attention for a time, but it will not attain the status of a standard design unless it is supported by the people. The common people appear to be ignorant, but they have an aesthetic common sense formed by tradition. I am confident that fine design will live on into the future.

# TITLES IN THE SERIES

Although the individual books in the series are designed as self-contained units, so that readers may choose subjects according to their personal interests, the series itself constitutes a full survey of Japanese art and will be of increasing reference value as it progresses. The following titles are listed in the same order, roughly chronological, as those of the original Japanese editions. Those marked with an asterisk (*) have already been published or will appear shortly. It is planned to publish the remaining titles at about the rate of eight a year, so that the English-language series will be complete in 1975.

1. Major Themes in Japanese Art, by Itsuji Yoshikawa
*2. The Beginnings of Japanese Art, by Namio Egami
*3. Shinto Art: Ise and Izumo Shrines, by Yasutada Watanabe
*4. Asuka Buddhist Art: Horyu-ji, by Seiichi Mizuno
5. Nara Buddhist Art: Todai-ji, by Takeshi Kobayashi
6. The Silk Road and the Shoso-in, by Ryoichi Hayashi
*7. Temples of Nara and Their Art, by Minoru Ooka
*8. Art in Japanese Esoteric Buddhism, by Takaaki Sawa
9. Heian Temples: Byodo-in and Chuson-ji, by Toshio Fukuyama
*10. Painting in the Yamato Style, by Saburo Ienaga
*11. Sculpture of the Kamakura Period, by Hisashi Mori
*12. Japanese Ink Painting: Shubun to Sesshu, by Ichimatsu Tanaka
*13. Feudal Architecture of Japan, by Kiyoshi Hirai
14. Momoyama Decorative Painting, by Tsuguyoshi Doi
*15. Japanese Arts and the Tea Ceremony, by T. Hayashiya, M. Nakamura, and S. Hayashiya
*16. Japanese Costume and Textile Arts, by Seiroku Noma
*17. Momoyama Genre Painting, by Yuzo Yamane
*18. Edo Painting: Sotatsu and Korin, by Hiroshi Mizuo
*19. The Namban Art of Japan, by Yoshitomo Okamoto
20. Edo Architecture: Katsura and Nikko, by Naomi Okawa
*21. Traditional Domestic Architecture of Japan, by Teiji Itoh
*22. Traditional Woodblock Prints of Japan, by Seiichiro Takahashi
*23. Japanese Painting in the Literati Style, by Yoshiho Yonezawa and Chu Yoshizawa
*24. Modern Currents in Japanese Art, by Michiaki Kawakita
25. Japanese Art in World Perspective, by Toru Terada
*26. Folk Arts and Crafts of Japan, by Kageo Muraoka and Kichiemon Okamura
*27. The Art of Japanese Calligraphy, by Yujiro Nakata
*28. The Garden Art of Japan, by Masao Hayakawa
*29. The Art of Japanese Ceramics, by Tsugio Mikami
30. Japanese Art: A Cultural Appreciation, by Saburo Ienaga

*The "weathermark" identifies this book as a production of John Weatherhill, Inc., publishers of fine books on Asia and the Pacific. Supervising editor: Armins Nikovskis. Book design and typography: Meredith Weatherby. Layout of illustrations: Sigrid Nikovskis. Production supervisor: Yutaka Shimoji. Composition: General Printing Co., Yokohama. Color-plate engraving and printing: Mitsumura Printing Co., Tokyo and Benrido Printing Co., Kyoto. Monochrome letterpress platemaking and printing and text printing: Toyo Printing Co., Tokyo. Binding: Makoto Binderies, Tokyo. The typeface used is Monotype Baskerville, with hand-set Optima for display.*